GOD'S TRANSFORMING LOVE

Daily Reflections on His Life Changing Power

LLOYD JOHN OGILVIE

Regal Books
A Division of GL Publications
Ventura, California, U.S.A.

Published by Regal Books
A Division of GL Publications
Ventura, California 93006
Printed in U.S.A.

The meditations comprising this book were selected by the editors as being
among the best of Dr. Ogilvie's writings in his several Regal books.

Library of Congress Cataloging-in-Publication Data

Ogilvie, Lloyd John.
   God's transforming love.

   Bibliography: p.
   1. Devotional exercises. I. Stewart, Ed. II. Title.
BV4832.2.039   1988   242   88-11393
ISBN 0-8307-1189-9

1 2 3 4 5 6 7 8 9 10/ 92 91 90 89 88

Rights for publishing this book in other languages are contracted by Gospel
Literature International (GLINT) foundation. GLINT also provides technical
help for the adaptation, translation, and publishing of Bible study resources
and books in scores of languages worldwide. For further information, contact
GLINT, Post Office Box 488, Rosemead, California, 91770, U.S.A., or the
publisher.

Contents

GOD'S TRANSFORMING LOVE

He Fills My Emptiness

Our emotional needs are part of our created nature. God made us that way. We were created for a relationship with Him. Only fellowship with God can fill the emptiness of our emotional natures.

LET GOD MEET YOUR EMOTIONAL NEEDS

Praise be to the God and Father of our Lord Jesus Christ! In his great mercy he has given us new birth into a living hope through the resurrection of Jesus Christ from the dead. 1 Peter 1:3, *NIV*

There are four deep, undeniable emotional needs we all have in common. We may be packaged differently in the wrappings of a unique individuality, but beneath the trimmings we are all the same on the emotional level. We all need to be *loved,* to feel *forgiven,* to experience *security* and to sense an adequate *hope* for the future. All of our other emotional needs for acceptance, esteem, affirmation, freedom and purposefulness flow from these basic four.

One of the most alarming realizations of life is that other people cannot satisfy these needs. No one can love us as much as we need to be loved. No person can give us an adequate experience of forgiveness. Security does not come from people or circumstances. Hope must spring from something more than another person's assurance that everything will work out and we should not worry.

Our emotional needs are part of our created nature. God made us that way. We were created for a relationship with Him. Only fellowship with God can fill the emptiness of our emotional natures. The gospel is not only truth about God, it is the offer of a new relationship with Him, ourselves and others which fulfills our emotional needs.

It is true that nothing can be in our hearts that has not first been in our heads. But if what's in our thinking does not reach our feelings, we will not be able to live the abundant life Jesus offers. He said that we were to know the truth and the truth would set us free. We not only need to get our heads straight, we need to get our feelings sorted out.

It is on the emotional level that most of us are blocked. Some of us have emotional malnutrition as a result of an inadequate experience of love in our childhood or present families and find it difficult to give to others what we have not experienced ourselves. Others of us have felt rejection or the excruciating pain of broken relationships. Still others are racked with the memory of past failures, the inability to forgive ourselves and try again. And then, all of us at times feel the turbulent emotions of anger, impatience, fear and frustration. Often we don't know what to do with these feelings. Repression results in depression. Explosion results in confusion. There must be some alternative.

Getting our feelings sorted out is crucial not only for

ourselves, but for all the people around us. It's not a simple matter; only God can do it. And that brings us to the foot of the cross. It is there that the love, forgiveness, security and hope we so desperately need flow in limitless, unreserved power. Charles Spurgeon once said that "there are some sciences that may be learned by the head, but the science of Christ crucified can only be learned by the heart."

We need to be loved. The cross tells us that God loves us and will not let us go. It is an authoritative love from the Creator and Ruler of the universe. It is an unmotivated love flowing from His pleasure in us in spite of what we have done or been. It is an unqualified love which cannot be dissuaded. It is a liberating love which sees us "perfect" in Christ, not in our imperfections. That is the healing we all need. The result is new acceptance of ourselves and an exuberant burst of love for others.

We need to be forgiven. We all fail. The emotions of regret, remorse and self-incrimination lead to discouragement and despair. Then the cross breaks through and we are forgiven. Nothing will ever change that. The past is blotted out; the present is cleansed; the future is delivered of the fear of failure. When we do sin, we need to grasp the truth that we were forgiven even before it happened! The result is liberation from the syndrome of repeated sin.

We need security. The cross is the foundation of assurance. We become secure only in the presence of an unchanging love. We have a confidence that emotional pressures cannot assail. We are stable and steadfast on the Rock of Ages, our firm foundation:

"How firm a foundation, ye saints of the Lord, is laid for your faith in his excellent Word! What more can he say than to you he hath said, you who to Jesus for refuge have fled?"[1]

9

We need hope. Emotional maturity is the result of a confidence for the future that is ours in the hope of the gospel.

Getting our failings sorted out begins with these four stabilizing emotions. In that context we can get in touch with our feelings.

How do you feel right now? Up, down, joyous, sad, angry, cold, warm, hostile or peaceful? However you feel, own up to the feeling. Then refocus on the cross. Into the depths of your emotions will flow the healing love, forgiveness, security and hope that will transform how you feel about yourself, life, others and your responsibilities.

"Bless the Lord, O my soul: and all that is within me, bless his holy name. Bless the Lord, O my soul, and forget not all his benefits" (Ps. 103:1,2,*KJV*).

Especially forget not the cross!

Giver of love, forgiveness, security and hope, I revel in the knowledge that you emptied yourself at the cross in order to fill my deepest needs. I am full and content in you today.

PEACE
PUTS PEOPLE
TOGETHER

And the peace of God, which transcends all
understanding, will guard your hearts and
your minds in Christ Jesus.
Philippians 4:7, *NIV*

There's a boy in my congregation who shares my love for words. He tries to stump me with the challenge to spell and define new words he's discovered. To my dismay and—a few times—embarrassment, he's come up with some words that I didn't know were in the dictionary, and a few others, I later found out, were not. Like some adults, he gets the wrong word in the right place or a right word in the wrong place.

Recently he led me down a primrose path of conversation to set me up for the use of a word he'd learned—or so he thought! He asked me if I knew a word based on a Latin word to describe a person who is active or skilled in practical affairs. While I thought, he added that it also was used for the scientific evolution of causes and effects. Before I could say the word, he said, "I'm a very fragmatic person you know!" He meant pragmatic. We both laughed when I explained the difference; but I thanked him for coining a new word.

A "fragmatic" person! The phrase describes many of us and what's happening to us. We are scattered people, flying off in all directions. But the problem is more profound than the pressure of too much to do or a multiplicity of competing loyalties. We are "fragmatic" in our nature. The unity of mind, soul, emotion, will and body has been wrenched apart. We long to be made whole as we were meant to be. The explosion of man's nature, begun in Adam's rebellion against God, is still detonating, sending the shrapnel of our persons in every direction.

Perhaps this is the reason there is so much talk about wholeness today. Physicians are discovering that they must treat the whole person and have developed what's called holistic medicine. Eminent internists at long last are investigating the deeper causes of some sickness in the mental and spiritual dis-ease of patients. Oncologists are busy these days plumbing the depths of the interrelationship of stress and some forms of cancer. Psychiatrists are becoming aware that you can't heal emotional disorders without remedial care for a person's body, spirit, relationships and environment. Theologians are finally showing a reverence for more than conceptualized belief and are devoting time to the implications of right thinking for emotional health and relational integration.

Spiritual leaders have had to face the fact that many people who are "saved" are still emotional cripples who need the healing of memories or the liberation of their wills to act on what they believe. It is an exciting time of discovering a very basic truth: a human being is a unity. All the person-healing disciplines are realizing that they cannot deal with one aspect of the complex nature of a person without care for the whole person.

Our word "whole" comes from the Anglo-Saxon word *hal,* meaning whole, completeness, or integration. The source of wholeness is peace. The Greek word for "peace," *eirene,* means more than tranquility or absence of outer conflict. The word implies a knitting together of what has been fragmented. Peace is the Lord's healing of the "fragmatist." It results in the perfect unity of all the factors of our humanity.

Peace is the gift of Calvary. The strife and enmity between God and man caused by sin, has been dealt with in a-once-and-for-all, complete atonement. Peace is made between God and those who will accept the free gift of forgiveness, reconciliation and love through the blood of the cross. There is no hope of wholeness until we are reunited with our Lord through the imputed righteousness we have through the Lamb of God, Christ our sacrifice. When we are pulled apart by rebellion and the arrogant desire to run our own lives, we are fractured from the centering power which can pull us together.

A question begs consideration: Why are there so few Christians who are whole? The reason is that many of us have resisted His invasion into all the aspects of our nature. It is possible to believe that Jesus is the Christ and still be a fragmented person. There are conceptual Christians whose faith has not penetrated emotion, will or body. Also there are emotional Christians who need to get their thinking straight as well as volitional Christians who are willing to do what's right without the power to do it. And there are others who need to discover how to express

13

their faith in their physical lives. The body's habits, disabilities or passions must be brought under the control of the Spirit. Instead of being fragmented into pieces, we can know the peace of the harmonious functioning of our total nature under His Lordship. The peace of Christ enables wholeness.

———————◇———◇—◇———————

Lord, you were broken at Calvary that I might be a whole person today. Thank you for prevailing, penetrating peace.

THE ART OF GRACE- FULL LIVING

To the praise of his glorious grace, which he
has freely given us in the One he loves.
Ephesians 1:6, *NIV*

I f I had to select one word to describe the nature of God
it would be grace. The word flashes like a diamond held
up to the light. It means giving, forgiving, unchanging,
unmotivated, unconditional love.

God relates to us with accepting and affirming love.
The cross is the sublime expression of that unqualified
love. Before we were ready, deserving, worthy, Christ
died for us.

The apostle Paul never could forget that grace. It was
the ethos of his thinking, the ambience of his living, the

15

motivation of his ministry. Grace for Paul meant to live in Christ and allow Christ to live in him. One enabled him to receive the blessing of Christ's message, death and resurrection. The other filled his being with the indwelling Christ Himself. The first without the last could not have produced the powerful man Paul became. The secret was that Christ actually took up residence in him.

The greatest need in the Church today is for those of us who have believed in Christ to be filled with Him. An authentic person is one who is being transformed into His image. The more we experience His amazing grace, the more we can yield our minds and hearts to be His post-resurrection home. Each of the problems we face are a prelude to fresh grace. They bring us to the end of ourselves and to the place of openness in which He can fill us with Himself. The tissues of our brain can be agents of thinking His thoughts, our emotions can be channels of His warmth and love.

Each time we read the message of grace in the Scriptures, whenever we hear it preached or taught, or when its precious healing balm is offered to us by another who has experienced it afresh, we are given new release and power. Our hunger for grace is never satisfied. God made it so. He created us so that we could live by love alone. Whatever else we accomplish or achieve is empty without it.

Paul learned that repeatedly. The Lord's word to him was, "My grace is sufficient for you, for My strength is made perfect in weakness" (2 Cor. 12:9, *NKJV*). The apostle discovered that the Lord Himself was the answer to times of seemingly unanswered prayer. The Lord never gives us anything that will separate us from Him. But there are things which we do that block out our capacity to receive grace.

16

There is nothing more crippling than our efforts to be adequate in our own strength. After we accept Christ as our Savior, we often try to live the Christian life for Christ rather than by His indwelling power. That's the essential cause of the impotence of most Christians and churches today. We soon lose our authenticity in pretense of blind allegiance to traditions, rules or regulations. That puts us on our Damascus Road heading on a collision course with the Savior. What Paul did with his fanatic zeal for the law, we do for our own self-induced striving to be good enough to be loved for our piety. It is strange how we twist the free gift of grace and try to earn what is ours already!

But the exciting thing which I see happening today is that religious people are being set free from that. We are discovering with Paul that Christ's grace is indeed sufficient.

I talked to a pastor of a church in the East. He was bogged down in leading a difficult parish of traditional church men and women. I asked him if he could ask for one gift for his people what it would be.

The pastor's answer was very revealing. "I'd ask for what I need as much as they do. An excitement about Christ—a supernatural church in which He is given full reign to change lives and give us the freedom to love and be loved."

The response was on target, but required that he begin with himself. We talked for hours about his life. There were memories to be healed, sins to be forgiven, an impossible relationship in his life to be transformed. The man needed to hear the simple message of grace, and experience it in a new way. Our conversation ended on our knees, pouring out to God the emptiness the man felt. Then we prayed to accept the gift of peace for his turbulent heart.

My reason for telling this man's story is because of what happened through him when he returned to his parish. He determined to preach grace for a year. He returned to Christ-centered, cross-oriented preaching. A fire of grace was burning in his own spirit as he talked about the cross, the new life in Christ, the power of the indwelling Christ, and the adventure of being grace-motivated lovers of people. There was boldness, freedom, joy. One by one his officers joined him in his search for authentic Christianity. Then the fire of Pentecost began to spread throughout the congregation.

I talk to members of the laity everywhere who have found new life in Christ by submitting their fears and failures to His grace. Recently a woman said, "I've been a church member for years, but it wasn't until my arrogant religiosity was broken by an unsolvable problem in a relationship with my son that I had to go back to the cross for grace to sustain me. It's amazing! The basic message that Christ loves me and can take the broken pieces of this mess and make something out of it gave me hope and peace."

The great thing about this woman's recovery of grace is that once she surrendered her need and saw Christ at work, she became a very gracious person. The Lord has used her repeatedly in helping others with similar problems. Her self-satisfied, aloof judgmentalism was transformed by grace.

I know grace in my own life. My experience of Christ began when friends explained to me the wonder of His grace. My whole Christian experience through more than 40 years of knowing the Savior has been a never-ending growth in grace. Some time during each day I am brought back to the fact of the cross.

I can readily agree with Charles G. Finney, "A state of

mind that sees God in everything is evidence of growth in grace and a thankful heart."

I don't understand all the whys and hows of your grace, loving Lord. But I know my activities are futile unless they are "graced" by your presence and touch. Grace me afresh today!

LEARNING
TO LIVE
INSIDE OUT

Christ in your hearts is your only hope of glory. Colossians 1:27, *TLB*

―――――――――◇―――◆―――◇―――――――――

C hrist in us is the hope of glory. Glory is the manifestation of Christ. Our hope of His manifest ministry is in Him alone. That means that we become like Him in attitude, action and reaction. Our words and nonverbal communication can be His to others. The *Living Bible* paraphrase of Colossians 1:26,27 catches this: "He has kept this secret for centuries and generations past, but now at last it has pleased him to tell it to those who love him and live for him, and the riches and glory of his plan are for you Gentiles too. And this is the secret: *that Christ in your hearts is your only hope of glory.*"

This experience of the indwelling Christ has transformed both my personal life and my ministry. When I was gripped by this liberating experience it set me free from compulsive efforts to earn my status with God by being good enough. It replenished the parched places of my soul that kept my Christian life a constant dry spell. The indwelling Christ gave me all that I had previously worked to achieve, studied to understand, struggled to accomplish.

It happened when I realized that I had a purpose without power. After a few years in the ministry I was exhausted and frustrated. My preaching was biblically oriented and Christ-centered, but few lives were moved or changed. My church was well organized and highly programmed, but there was neither love nor joy among the people. Most of all, I was aware that something was wrong; something was lacking. Years of theological education and biblical exposition had hit wide of the mark of the most crucial truth the Word contained. In my discouragement and despair, I asked Christ to tell me what was wrong.

My personal devotions, kept regularly but fruitlessly up to that time, were in John and Colossians. One day I was led to read Christ's promise that He could make His home with us (see John 14:23). Then I read these words in Colossians: "Christ in you, the hope of glory" (1:27, *KJV*). They sounded like a trumpet blast. "That's it!" I said. I had tried to follow Christ to the best of my ability. I was a man "in Christ" as a recipient of the gift of His death and resurrection for me. I knew that I was forgiven, that death had no power over me and that I was alive forever. But now I was stunned intellectually with a truth I had missed. I was stirred emotionally by a power I had not appreciated. And most of all, I was startled by a vision of what the Christian

21

was meant to be: the dwelling place of Christ; the glorious riverbed of the flowing streams of the living Lord!

I got on my knees and prayed:

Lord, I've missed the secret. I have been ministering for you and have not allowed you to work through me. Come live your life in me. Love through me; forgive through me; suffer for the estranged through me; continue fresh realizations of Calvary everywhere about me.

The result of that prayer is that I discovered guidance is not something I go to Christ to receive, but something He signals from within my mind and spirit.

Each person I met or worked with gave me a fresh opportunity to let go and allow Christ to speak and love through me. I found, and continually rediscover now, that my task is only to pray for openness to let Him through, and then to marvel at what He says and does.

Problems and difficulties are gifts for new levels of depth in experiencing the limitless adequacy of what Christ can do. What a relief it is to no longer feel that I have to find answers and solve problems to please or placate Him. He is at work in me. I know that as surely as I feel my heart beat and my lungs breathe.

But don't misread my enthusiasm. I am not suggesting that there has been no pain or suffering. The difference is that there is less of the excruciating distress caused by my previous resistance to Him, and more of the realization that the difficulties of living are but the focus of the next phase of the penetration of the power of the cross.

Our responsibility is not only faithfulness but also relinquishment. The liberating insight is that wherever and with whomever His grace is needed, Christ is at work. If He lives in us it follows that He will lead us into those situations and to those people who need Him most. It isn't that we discern what Christ is doing and join Him—that's a mediocre level of discipleship—but rather, it is that, when Christ takes up residence in us, He leads us into places and to people in which He can use our lives as an extension of the Incarnation.

Lord, I am ready now to be your manifest intervention in situations to infuse joy, affirm growth or absorb pain and aching anguish. I plan to live this day and the rest of my life in the reality of you in me. Thank you for making it so!

LET GOD
MANAGE YOUR
COMFORT
ZONE

And I will pray the Father, and he shall give you another Comforter, that he may abide with you forever. John 14:16, *KJV*

The motto of the newspaperman, Joseph Pulitzer, owed much to Jesus: "Comfort the afflicted and afflict the comfortable." Jesus does just that! He comforts those who mourn over their own, others, and the world's suffering. The Greek word for comfort means "to call to the side of." Christ stands by our side when we become sensitive to the needs of our world and our part in it. When we become comfortable in any other security than Him, He unsettles us with His disturbing exposure of what life was meant to be.

Only Christ knows when we need to be comforted and

24

and when to alarm. Our own judgment of our needs is often wrong. When we think we need comforting, He often comes with a disturbing challenge which gets us on our feet. Then, too, when we do not know our need for fortification, He builds us up in love to face some imminent difficulty we must go through.

The wonderful good news is that He stands beside us. The Messiah was called the Comforter. Jesus promised to return in the power of the Holy Spirit, the Comforter. He comforts us by helping us to get a perspective on what we face, to see what He is teaching us in it, to learn what He can do with a life surrendered to Him and to experience the power of His sustaining Spirit. The comfort of Christ is the unlimited source of our courage.

There is a powerful story told of Leonardo da Vinci. One day in his studio he started work on a large canvas. He labored on it, choosing the subject carefully, arranging the perspective, sketching the outline, applying the colors and developing the background. Then, for some unknown reason, he stopped with the painting still unfinished. He called one of his students and asked him to finish. The student was flabbergasted. How could he finish a painting by one of the world's truly great masters? He protested his inadequacy and insufficiency for so challenging a task.

But the great artist silenced him. "Will not what I have done inspire you to do your best?" he asked.

That is really Jesus' question, isn't it? He began it all 2,000 years ago. His life, message, death, resurrection and living presence started the great painting of the redemption of the world. He has given us the task to finish the painting. But there is a difference. Da Vinci left his student alone; Jesus never does that. He has given us the color palette, and whispers His guiding insight to us at each uncertain stroke. We cannot shrink from the task. The challenge and inspiration press us on.

We sometimes get bogged down in the daily routine of living and forget the essential task of our life. We are part of a new breed of humanity. The Church is to be a new kind of society of love and forgiveness. Our task is nothing less than the changing and transformation of the world, beginning with ourselves, our families and our sphere of influence. In Christ we are given our image of true living. We are to know the same power and peace manifested in His life. What He has done and who He is inspires us to get on with the painting today with the Master's touch close at hand.

Who understands better than you, Lord, my failings, frustrations and fears? Thank you for your abiding, comforting presence which spurs me beyond myself to the me you've called me to be.

POWER OVER IMPOSSIBILITIES

Strengthened with all power according to his glorious might so that you may have great endurance and patience, and joyfully giving thanks to the Father.
Colossians 1:11,12, NIV

This is one of my favorite verses in the New Testament. I have repeated it at times of trial and challenge. It helps me remember that my fatigue, inadequacy and limitation can be replaced with the power of the Holy Spirit. When I feel empty and done in because I have come to the end of my resources, I now can thank God because I know that it is in a time like this that I receive the energizing strength of the Spirit. My prayer is that I will realize the inexhaustibility of the Lord all of the time, not just when I am at the end of my tether. And it's happening. What Paul prayed for the Colossians has

27

become the indefatigable reservoir for me.

To be strengthened with all power means "empowered with all power"—enabling power—uplifting, engendering, energizing power. The reason for this is that the power we experience is from the "glorious might" of God Himself. The liberating secret of triumphant living is that we were never meant to have adequate resources to do God's work on our own. It's ludicrous to try. We cannot love, forgive, care, nor make a difference in people's lives and our world on our own strength. Power is given to do those things we could never do alone.

The reason I lived for so long without realizing the power of the Holy Spirit is that I was attempting only those things which I could easily do on my own strength. One day a friend asked me what I was daring to do that only God's power could accomplish. I was alarmed to discover that my life was limited, cautious and fearful.

The adventure of Christianity began when I moved beyond self-reliance to dare to attempt those guided impossibilities that only the Lord could achieve. It was then that I knew what Paul meant by "glorious might." The Greek word is *kratos*, meaning "perfect strength." It is glorious in that it belongs to God, is a manifestation of His Spirit and is intended to bring honor to Him, not to me as the channel.

There are three great gifts which are ours when we are empowered with all power: endurance, patience and joy. We need all three. The order in the Greek text puts patience first. A. T. Robertson, in his *Word Pictures in the New Testament*, helped me to understand that patience as it is used here relates to perseverance, a brave patience a Christian can use to contend with various hindrances, persecutions and temptations which confront him. The Greek word *hupomone*, "patience," means to remain under difficulties while empowered by the situational strength of the Holy Spirit.

Endurance, or long-suffering as it is translated in some versions, means patience applied to relationships with people. The Spirit enables a capacity to relate to people with the endurance of God. Endurance does not retaliate, is not easily provoked to spiteful anger and tolerates rejection and injury. Both endurance and patience result from an experience of God's gracious love. When we realize what He has forgiven in us, we can forgive; when we are able to see people and situations from His perspective, we can trust Him, and love people as they are and in spite of what they do.

The outward manifestation of this inner grace is joy. Joy, *chara,* flows from grace, *charis.* When we know that we are loved and cherished be God, joy floods our emotions. It is far superior to happiness, which is dependent on circumstances and people. Joy is love growing in the soil of difficulties and suffering.

Lord, I need patience, endurance and joy today—daily life is flat and tedious without them. By faith, I fuel up at the power tank of your glorious might for an overcoming day.

DEALING WITH DECISIONS

May the God of peace . . . make you
complete in every good work to do His will,
working in you what is well pleasing in His
sight. Hebrews 13:20,21, *NKJV*

A friend of mine called to arrange a visit over lunch. "I really need to talk with you," he said urgently. "I've got to make a crucial decision about a job offer I have. It could be the most important career decision of my life. My need is for an objective person to listen and tell me how to make a right decision."

I told him I'd be happy to listen and share what I'd learned over the years about discovering God's specific will for particular decisions.

30

When we got together I quickly discovered that the young executive was very serious about wanting to know God's will for the important decision he had to make. He opened the conversation in earnest. "I don't want to make a wrong choice," he said. "But how do I know for sure what is God's will? I really want to take this job, but what if that's just my will and not the Lord's will for me?"

I replied with some questions. "Can you think of any reason the Lord would not want you to make this a yes decision? Will you be asked to do anything contrary to what you believe? Can you continue to put the Lord first in your life if you take this job? Will this opportunity bring you closer to your life goals professionally? Will it give you a chance to witness for your faith? Can you claim the Lord's presence and power as you do your work?"

He could answer all the questions affirmatively.

"When do you have to give an answer to the offer?" I asked.

He told me he had a few days.

Then I suggested an exercise in prayer that has worked for me in making decisions. "It sounds like you really want to take this job. Why not try that on for the days between now and when you must respond. Live with a yes decision. Ask the Lord to create a conviction of rightness or wrongness. Open yourself in prayer. Yield your mind to Him, surrender your will specifically for this, and ask Him to use everything—circumstances, people you trust, and the Scriptures—to affirm or negate your decision."

A few days later the man called me to tell me that he felt guided to take the job. "I was so concerned," he said. "I thought that because I wanted this, God was probably against it. I couldn't imagine that He would be for me in this!"

I reminded him that the Lord was his friend and wanted what was best for him. He had guided the whole process. Because the man was open to allow the Lord to condition his thoughts, he had been given clear direction. In this case all signals were go!

Decisions, decisions. We all face them every day. Some are insignificant; others are crucial for our future. In all of them we want to make guided choices. We long to know and do the Lord's will.

The question I'm asked most often is, How can I know the will of God? The question exposes people's inconsistent communion with the Lord.

My answer is not to give people a set of rules to finding God's will but to explain His promise to work in us constantly so that we are ready for the choices of life. That leads to the discipline of prayer, not just for crises, but in daily times of listening and constant communion through the day. That's often more than people bargain for who raise the question about how to know God's will.

Over the years, I have discovered that the Lord does not distribute cheap grace and guidance. He created us for a consistent companionship and redeemed us to live in close oneness with Him. Those who rush to Him only when a decision demands His help are often made to wait. He uses the time of indecision to draw us closer to Him and establish a profound relationship which will prepare us for decisions in the future.

I have a friend who calls her doctor only when she has an illness. She talks to him on the phone and wants a prescription of some miracle drug for whatever malady she has. Consistently, she has resisted general checkups and the doctor's desire to help her with an overall plan of diet, exercise and health care which would avert her repeated illnesses. Recently he refused to give quickie remedies on the phone and told her she must submit to his comprehensive program of remedial care for her long-range well-being. That would necessitate more than a phone call in crises. The doctor cared too much for this woman's health to continue as a telephone prescription service.

How much more the Lord wants to maximize our spiritual lives. He is up to momentous things with us. In His master plan for the kingdom in our time, He has plans for each of us which fit into His overall will. The people around us, the church of which we are a part, the places we work and the communities in which we live are dependent on our seeking the Lord's will consistently, so that His maximum in every area can be accomplished. When we are out of touch with Him, we make wrong choices, develop unguided programs and head in directions that are less than He envisions for us. We and others, as well as situations in which we are involved, are cheated.

Hebrews 13:20-21 sounds a trumpet call. The continuing ministry of Christ, God with us, is the focus of this triumphant benediction. Through Him we are participants of the new covenant in His blood. A covenant is a promise. We are covenant members of the new Israel through Christ. Our relationship is based on the grace offered us through the cross.

The Lord has called us to be His people and will not let us go. As He took responsibility for our redemption, He assumes the initiative role in "making us complete." The word for "complete" in this stirring passage is *katatisai*, from *katartizo*, meaning "to equip." The Lord equips us to do His will. As indwelling Lord living in us He gives us whatever we need to know and do His will. He wants us to do what is "well pleasing in His sight."

But He does not leave that for us to flounder about until we happen on it. He readily responds to our willing-

33

ness and makes His will known for each situation, choice, and decision. To do that He equips us with the gifts of wisdom, knowledge, discernment, and vision.

I rejoice, Wise Father, in my growing relationship with you through which I find daily direction into your will. And so again today, guide me, O thou great Jehovah!

NO ROOM FOR THE DEVIL

Then I will dwell in your midst.
Zechariah 2:11, *NASB*

You and I were created to be the containers and communicators of the Spirit of God. That was God's original intention. We were meant to be the dwelling place of God. He is the tenant who owns the house. But sin evicted Him. Rebellion slammed the door in His face.

That's why Jesus came. God with us, creating a new breed of people in whom He could live. God dwelt in Jesus to call a new Israel to be His home. "And the Word became flesh, and dwelt among us, and we beheld His glory, glory as of the only begotten from the Father, full of grace and truth" (John 1:14, *NASB*). The ancient prophecy was realized. "Then I will dwell in your midst" (Zech. 2:11, *NASB*).

But we know what happened. "He came to His own, and those who were His own did not receive Him" (John 1:11, *NASB*).

And so Jesus turned to the common people to create a new Israel. They heard Him gladly. The disciples responded with ready receptiveness. "But as many as received Him, to them He gave the right to become children of God, even to those who believe in His name, who were born not of blood, nor of the will of the flesh, nor of the will of man, but of God" (John 1:12,13 *NASB*).

On the last night of His ministry before He was crucified, Jesus unveiled the liberating secret of how the empty house was to be filled. "If anyone loves Me, he will keep My word; and My Father will love him, and We will come to him, and make Our abode with him" (John 14:23, *NASB*). Then He went on: "Abide in Me, and I in you. As the branch cannot bear fruit of itself, unless it abides in the vine, so neither can you, unless you abide in me" (John 15:4, *NASB*).

Pentecost became the triumphant climax of the Incarnation. As the Spirit of God had dwelt in Jesus, now through His death and resurrection the original purpose of creation had been reclaimed. The empty, receptive hearts of the apostles were filled with the Holy Spirit. God had made His home in them. Each new challenge brought fresh infilling, the remarkable lives we see spread across the pages of the book of Acts.

Eventually the dynamic of the Spirit-filled life spread to Saul of Tarsus. His persecution of the Christians forced him to observe their amazing power. It was Stephen's dying witness that shattered open the windows of his haunted heart. Saul was ready when he encountered the

Lord Himself on the road to Damascus. Then through Ananias, whom he had come to imprison, the Pharisee was set free from the prison of his own powerless religiosity. After years of Spirit-filled living, the apostle Paul did more than any other Christian in history to put into writing the distilled essence of God's original purpose for His people.

To the Epehsians he wrote his deepest longing for all people. "For this reason, I bow my knees before the Father, from whom every family in heaven and on earth derives its name, that He would grant you, according to the riches of His glory, to be strengthened with power through His Spirit in the inner man; so that Christ may dwell in your hearts through faith" (Eph. 3:14-17, *NASB*). Paul knew that the Christians' most difficult battle was not against flesh and blood, but "against the powers, against the world forces of this darkness, against the spiritual forces of wickedness in the heavenly places" (Eph. 6:12, *NASB*).

Paul took Satan and his demonic emissaries seriously. From his own life he had learned that the only antidote to demon possession was the Spirit-filled life. The empty heart had to be filled. That accounts for the urgency of the Apostle's message about the Spirit to the Christians at Rome. "However, you are not in the flesh but in the Spirit, if indeed the Spirit of God dwells in you. But if anyone does not have the Spirit of Christ, he does not belong to Him. And if Christ is in you, though the body is dead because of sin, yet the spirit is alive because of righteousness. But if the Spirit of Him who raised Jesus from the dead dwells in you, He who raised Christ Jesus from the dead will also give life to your mortal bodies through His Spirit who indwells you" (Rom. 8:9-11, *NASB*).

The full impact of the Spirit-filled life as the protection

against the invasion of Satan is given by Paul to the Colossians. They too had had their bouts with Ol' Scratch. "Christ in you, the hope of glory" (Col. 1:27, *NASB*) is the secret mystery of the Christian's power over evil.

Being filled with you, Spirit of God, leaves no room for satanic intrusion. Fill me again to capacity and let me overflow to the empty ones I touch today.

GOD'S WINNING WAY IN YOU

Everyone born of God overcomes the world. This is the victory that has overcome the world, even our faith.
1 John 5:4, *NIV*

———————◆———————

When John wrote to the early Church, he wanted them to know that as long as life was focused on Christ, the Christians could overcome the world. The words for "overcome" and "victory" come from the same Greek word *nikao*. We have overcome the world when we lift our eyes from the things of earth and seek the things that are above. Then we can say "But thanks be to God! He gives us the victory through our Lord Jesus Christ" (1 Cor. 15:57, *NIV*).

The victorious life is ultimately based on our conviction of the Lord's second coming. He will return in glory. History is not an endless stream of eventualities. There will be a final triumph of the Lord in His return. We live by an undiminishable hope: "When Christ . . . appears, then you also will appear with him in glory" (Col. 3:4, *NIV*). That's all we need to know. The end is sure, and in the meantime, Clement of Alexandria was right: "Christ turns all our sunsets into dawns."

Some of us would have to admit that talk about the victorious life is disturbing. We believe in Christ's victory, but we don't feel very victorious. We know ourselves too well for that. There are thoughts, feelings, attitudes and habits which mock the reality of the victorious life in us. We are very aware of our impotence to change some of the things which still debilitate and defeat us. We are discouraged by our human nature.

The victorious life is constant and continuous. The Lord is never finished with us. But we must cooperate; He will not force the new nature on us. The things which rob us of knowledge and experiencing the victorious life must be surrendered to Him. The cycle of death and resurrection, commitment and liberation, is recapitulated over again with each aspect of our nature, attitudes and actions we entrust to Him.

If we don't feel victorious it's a sure sign we haven't claimed the power of Christ's victory for the specific things which rob us of joy and freedom. Before you turn this page or put this book down, you need to ask yourself, "What is it that makes me feel defeated or discouraged about myself and my relationship with others?" Don't generalize. Be definite.

Ask God to expose to you what got you locked on dead center. Then take them one by one and pray:

Gracious Lord, thank you for showing me what keeps me from the victorious life. I surrender it to you. I claim

Christ's defeat of that on Calvary, and accept the same power which raised Him from the dead to be different. Thank you for living your life in me. I give you complete control to make me the person you want me to be.

That prayer is itself a victory. The victorious life is on the way. Claim it for yourself right now and thank God for it continually!

———————————◇———◇———◇———————————

Thank you, Victorious Lord, for the prospect of being a winner in life every day because of you.

GOD'S TRANSFORMING LOVE

He Changes My Life

Any change in our personality must be a result of a transformation of the values, goals, feelings, attitudes, and self-esteem of the person who lives inside our skins.

ONCE I WAS LOST, BUT NOW I'M FOUND!

Suppose one of you has a hundred sheep and loses one of them. Does he not leave the ninety-nine in the open country and go after the lost sheep until he finds it?
Luke 15:4, *NIV*

Several summers ago I had a preaching engagement at the Tabernacle in Ocean City, New Jersey. My hotel room overlooked the Atlantic and the busy boardwalk which parallels the seaside. Thousands of people stroll or ride bicycles along the boardwalk and frequent the famous saltwater taffy shops or the amusement parks situated along the way.

From my room I could see the endless streams of people walking aimlessly. A blend of clattering voices and the carnival sounds of the merry-go-round wafted into my room on the soft, salty, humid, summer night's breeze. A pleasant background for my time of study in preparation for my sermon the next day. My mind was focused on Luke 15 and Jesus' parables of the lost sheep and the lost coin. I did not expect that what I was about to hear over one of the speakers which adorn the light posts along the boardwalk would bring what I was reading into stark reality.

Piercing through the din was an anonymous announcement. None of the people on the boardwalk seemed to hear, respond or care. But from my vantage the words were alarming, though the announcer's voice did not express the pathos and anguish of the distress.

"A little girl about five years old, answering to the name of Wendy, has been lost. She is wearing a yellow dress and carrying a teddy bear. She has brown eyes, auburn hair. Anyone knowing the whereabouts of Wendy, please report to the Music Pier. Her parents are waiting for her here."

I tried to return to my reading. But my mind was on Wendy. Who was she? Where was she now in what must have looked to her to be a forest of legs along the boardwalk? How did she feel without the clasp of her father's strong hand? I felt heart-wrenching empathy as I pictured her clutching her faithful teddy bear, tears streaming down her face, her heart bursting with fright and loneliness.

Then I pictured her parents. That triggered my own parental concerns and flooded me with memories of times my own children had gotten lost. I wanted to start a search party all my own or go wait with the parents. What must they be feeling? Imagine all the tragic things that could happen to Wendy: the sea, physical harm, strangers . . . .

I was deeply relieved when I learned that Wendy was

found. I pictured the thankful looks of love on the parents' faces and felt the joy they must have expressed. Warmth pulsated in my arms as I almost felt the tenderness of holding sobbing, little Wendy. I could hear something inside me saying, "It's all right now, Wendy. Don't cry any more. It's okay. We've found you. Never let go of my hand again. I love you, Wendy."

Then I looked out of my window again at the streams of humanity along the boardwalk. How many of them were lost and did not know it? Or how many felt a deep lostness inside and wished an announcement would be made about their spiritual condition? Did anyone care? I wondered how many of them knew that they needed a heavenly Father as much as Wendy needed her daddy.

What does it mean to be lost? Some who read this can feel the lostness of having no intimate relationship with God. We are lost indeed, when we have never felt the love of our Father, never accepted His forgiveness or experienced His indwelling Spirit. He is in search of us who, like sheep, have nibbled our way from the pasture, searching for new turf of satisfaction and adventure.

Others of us are lost in that we no longer desire the Shepherd to guide our lives. The desire to "make it on our own" has led us to other pastures. The inbred need for either the Shepherd or the flock is negated in our wandering hearts.

Still others of us have lost our direction. We feel lost in the multiplicity of alternatives. There is no clear conviction of where our lives are headed and how each challenge or opportunity fits into a greater plan.

Some of us feel the lostness of not being loved. That has bashed our self-esteem. We do not feel "special" to anyone, especially the significant people of our lives. The result is the lost condition of not loving ourselves.

Then there is the lost feeling of having failed and needing forgiveness and a new beginning. We feel unacceptable because of what we have said or done.

Everyone of us has felt the lost ache of broken relationships. Misunderstandings, differences, arguments, cutting words and sickening silences leave us hurting and cut off.

But by far the most tragic sense of lostness is not knowing we are lost. The undeniable evidence of that is lack of caring for those who are spiritually lost. When we become insensitive to the pain and perplexity of people who need the Savior, and when we have little else but judgmentalism and criticism for the mess people get into—then we are most in need of a loving Shepherd to find us and bring us back to life.

In what ways do you identify with the lost sheep? Jesus wants to know! He has left the ninety-nine and is searching for you and me.

Blaise Pascal, the seventeenth century philosopher, experienced the searching Shepherd when he heard His tender words, "Thou wouldst not be searching for me hadst I not already found thee." Any longing for God is because He has drawn near. The desire to know Him and recover the warm assurance of His presence is the result of His particularized, individual care for us. The sense of being found creates a desire to bring all the lost areas of relationships of life under His gracious care.

The Hound of Heaven was indefatigable in His relentless pursuit of Francis Thompson. Listen to the poet's plight.

I fled Him, down the nights and down the days;
I fled Him, down the arches of the years;
I fled Him, down the labyrinthine ways

Of my own mind; and in the mist of tears
I hid from Him, and under running laughter.
Up vistaed hopes I sped;
And shot, precipitated,
Adown Titanic glooms of chasmed fears.
From those strong Feet that followed,
    followed after.

The Shepherd's footfall is always there. He will not give us up. How can it be that He always knows where and how we are hiding? But skip down to the last stanza of Thompson's poem and hear the Shepherd say,

Ah, fondest, blindest, weakest
I am He Whom thou seekest![1]

It is true. All our longing, restlessness and discontent is because of our search for the One who has found us. Our lostness is healed when we accept the liberating comfort that we can never wander from Him. He does know and care! At this very moment He is surrounding us with accepting love. The Shepherd's staff is a cross!

As I closed the Bible that night in Ocean City, I too began to sing for joy. My heart was flooded with almost uncontainable exuberance about my Lord. Forty years ago I was lost. He found me in a college dormitory. There have been lost times when I let go of the Shepherd, but He never let go of me. In a wonderful way I knew He had found me again in that hotel room. The joy I experienced would last only as long as the lost on that boardwalk, or on the streets of Los Angeles, or in the pews of my church, or in the homes of my parish were my purpose and passion.

Before I fell asleep it seemed as if the Lord was saying, "Lloyd, if you want me, care for the lost. That's where you will find me. What you do for and with them, you will do for and with me!"

Seeking Shepherd, help me not to forget the agony of being lost without you or the ecstasy of being found by you. Use me in the continuing "search and rescue" ministry of other lost sheep.

NOTHING HAS CHANGED, BUT EVERYTHING IS DIFFERENT

Those who hope in the Lord will renew their strength. They will soar on wings like eagles; they will run and not grow weary, they will walk and not be faint.
Isaiah 40:31, *NIV*

O nce, in the same week, I had a power failure in my home and in my life. The first became symbolic of the second. A violent storm cut the power lines which had fed electricity to my neighborhood. We were without electricity for hours. The lights and appliances were totally inoperable.

As I stumbled about in the darkness I was tempted to blame the lamps and light bulbs. That made me think about how absurd it would be to go up to the refrigerator and kick it saying, "You dumb refrigerator, why don't you work?" It would have been equally unproductive to pound

51

the stove saying, "Why you inefficient, inadequate stove, why don't you do what you were manufactured to do?" In the same way I could not lambaste the air-conditioning system when it did not produce throughout the long, powerless night. A whole section of Los Angeles was without the energy we take for granted with a flick of a switch.

That same week I experienced an overload of the circuits in my spiritual life. I took on too much. My own concerns, worry over people and a humanly impossible schedule broke the circuits. So much that I was attempting to get done was only what I had determined was crucial.

Momentarily I forgot that there's enough time in any one day to do what the Lord wills us to do. Exhaustion set in. While doing a television taping I realized the overload was making me less than maximum. What was usually done with ease became arduous and difficult.

Living on my own resources proved to be very inefficient. The business of the previous days had shortened my devotional time and the pressures had distracted me enough so that I didn't draw on the divine energy I usually find so sufficient through moment-by-moment prayer through each responsibility.

In the midst of the spiritual power failure the electricity failure occurred in my home. The parable was so pointed it made me burst out laughing at myself. The feeling of being out of power spiritually had prompted me to fall back into an old pattern of self-incrimination. "Lloyd, what's the matter with you!? You're a producer. You're supposed to pour out work—speaking, writing, pastoring, communicating on television. Now get with it!"

Then, as I thought about the inadequacy of the light bulbs, refrigerator, stove and air-conditioning system without electricity, the Lord seemed to say, "My son, you were created to be a transmitter of me. You've blocked the flow of my Spirit by attempting more in this week than I guided and set as priorities. You've had a power failure just like your house. To do my will effectively, you must depend on me and the flow of my power."

Ever have a day, week or period like that? I suspect we all have. You may be experiencing a time of power failure right now as you read this. The solution, as I discovered repeatedly, is not to condemn ourselves but to reestablish the power hookup that profound prayer offers.

The night of the electricity failure I went to bed realizing what the deepest need in my life was. It was not to finish up all my tasks or get from under the burden of pressure. What I needed most of all was to open myself again to the power of the Spirit of the Lord. My prayer time before I went to sleep was a plea for the Lord to take over and do through me what He wanted done.

I slept serenely and peacefully.

My waking thought was amazing. It was so captivating that I got up and wrote it down. Seven words that helped me know that the power of the Lord was back on in my life: "Nothing has changed, but everything is different!"

My desk was still piled high with demanding tasks, the schedule was still full, people's needs still concerned me. But *I* was different. In the flow of the Holy Spirit power I could prioritize, work with freedom, and enjoy being used by the Lord. The power failure was over!

If my life is to be distinctively different today, Lord, it will only be because of your power energizing my thoughts, words and deeds. Surge through me, I pray!

ARE YOU A SANCTIFIED SAINT?

God has chosen you from the beginning for salvation through sanctification by the Spirit and faith in the truth.
2 Thessalonians 2:13, *NASB*

---

anctification is the process of becoming distinctly different. It is the miracle of a character transformation in which we become more and more like Christ. We were created for growth toward maturity in every facet of life. We can be more than we ever imagined possible. "Christ in you, the hope of glory" (Col. 1:27, *NASB*) would be a beautiful way of vividly describing the source and substance of sanctification.

One of my members who recently began our congregation's daily discipline of prayer and Bible study remarked, "I am shocked to discover how many of my

54

basic presuppositions are essentially nonbiblical. I am an intellectual and yet I'm still in kindergarten as far as knowing and living on the basis of the Bible and the Lord's guidance."

That man is being sanctified!

I wish the same could be said of a Christian leader who carries heavy responsibilities and has a large following. But he uses people. When they have served their purpose, he casts them aside. A concerned person remarked, "There's a terrible chink in his armor, a flaw in his personality. Great regions of his life have never been touched by Christ."

Sharing this insight with this leader was not easy. It took hours of building confidence before we could talk about it and seek Christ's healing. His skyrocketing career had left out sanctification. A breakthrough came when I was able to share how Christ has been enabling constant growth in my life. He is not finished with any of us, especially me. A friendship has grown with this leader in which we share our needs to grow and pray for each other.

A woman who came to me for counseling confessed a problem in her marriage. She had been a Christian for years and yet found relationships painfully difficult. She was insecure, unable to give herself to others and plagued with low self-esteem. She probably would have remained in her immaturity if a crisis in her marriage had not forced her to discover how to grow up emotionally in Christ.

The Up and Outer is a fascinating book by a friend and officer in our church, Fred Foster. He describes his release from alcoholism some years ago. His life went bump on bottom below bottom, not on skid row but in the plush offices of the New York advertising world and the expense-account luxury of elegant bars and compulsive drinking. He was transformed by a traumatic encounter with Christ. His account of what followed is exciting. As he began to pray, read the Bible, participate in deep-caring fellowship groups, Christ began the long process of reshaping the core of his personality. The years of growth have produced the dynamic man Fred is today.

Another example is an officer of an eastern church who was a negative, uptight, rules-and-regulations churchman. He blocked progress at every turn. People began to wonder how he ever got elected to serve on the church board. Fortunately his fellow officers loved him into a realization that his manipulative methods were not working any better at church than they were in his home or at his office. Gracious acceptance coupled with honest confrontation edged him off his plateau of resistance to growth. I met him at a conference when he was in the midst of his metamorphosis. He was excited about all he was discovering of the new person that Christ was liberating him to be.

Each month our church accepts many into membership who have attended our new-members classes. Many of them are new converts to Christ. I am gratified by their excitement about Christ and the church. The challenge is to help them know that the joy they are experiencing is only a taste of what the Lord has in store for them. It will not all be smooth and easy. The Lord will continue to penetrate until all of life is under His guidance and power.

A young actor who has been a Christian for a year caught the challenge of this. "I'm sure not what I was, nor am I what I will be!" he exclaimed. Not a bad definition of sanctification. The loving Father has His hand on the clay!

Perhaps you have been satisfied with your level of growth. And yet, are you really? I realize that I am asking you and me to be honestly analytical about our life in Christ. In what ways have we grown in this past month? What new discovery about Christ has reoriented our thinking and motivated new behavior? What have we discovered about ourselves that needs to be surrendered to our Lord's refining fire? He's not done with us. Thank Him for that! We are holy people—we belong to Him. We are growing in holiness—being made like Him. And the best is still to come. We are becoming distinctly different people. Now we can say,

> And every virtue we possess
> And every victory won
> And every thought of holiness
> Are His alone.

Thank you, Lord, for what I am today by your grace, and for what I shall be as your sanctifying work continues in me.

JESUS GIVES YOU PERSONALITY PLUS

The kingdom of heaven is like yeast that a woman took and mixed into a large amount of flour until it worked all through the dough. Matthew 13:33, *NIV*

I t's changed my personality!" That was the confident claim of a middle-aged entertainer who had just had a face-lift. She had gone to a world-renowned cosmetic surgeon. His artistry removed the lines that age and difficulties had plowed deeply into her cheeks. The bags under her eyes were gone. With a careful incision along her hairline, the surgeon was able to stretch out the furrows in her brow.

I had to acknowledge that the woman looked 15 years younger. The harried, pressured look her face had developed was gone.

"You look like a new woman!" I said, in affirmation of the pain and expense she had endured.

"I only hope I can stay that way!" she responded, in a concerned voice which contradicted her now smooth, china-doll face.

"What do you mean?" I asked, immediately sensing her anxiety about the possible impermanence of her mask-like, cosmetic transformation.

"Well, the surgeon tells me that plastic surgery and face-lifting will be lasting only if there is a change in my inner patterns of thought and emotions. He says that my face is an expression of my psyche, and that I'll look the way I did again in three years unless I learn how to live. He recommended I see a psychiatrist or a spiritual advisor, to get a soul-lift that will help me keep my face-lift."

Amazing! The surgery had altered the woman's appearance enough to give her a temporary, positive self-image, but it had not really changed her personality. It would take more than a new face to make her a new person. A change in her personality would have to wait for that.

Personality change is not easy. Most of us are what the patterning of learning and experience has made us. We are conditioned creatures. Most authorities say that once a person's personality is set by early training, example and molding, it cannot be changed.

Personality is the sum total of our individuality. It is the outward expression of the intrinsic person within each of us: that which constitutes, characterizes and distinguishes us. As the entire organization of our uniqueness, personality is the composite of our essential self—innate disposition, beliefs, convictions, impulses, desires, appetites and instincts.

The people around us know who we are through our

59

personalities. Personality is the observable I—that which others experience, relate and respond to in the dialogue and drama of life. It is the product of all that's happened to, around and within us. Environment, education, culture, significant people and experience have all had a sculpturing hand in the shaping of the clay of our personality. The people we want to emulate, as well as those we reject as influential examples, have contributed to our image of ourselves.

We are all in the process of developing our personalities around the picture of the person we envision ourselves to be. The person we are inside, however, will irrevocably control the personality we express outwardly to others. Any change in our personality must be a result of a transformation of the values, goals, feelings, attitudes and self-esteem of the person who lives inside our skins.

That's where Jesus begins. He can transform our personalities!

He never used the word. It cannot be found recorded in the Scriptures. And yet, everything Jesus said, did and does radically alters and reshapes personality. The Lord is deeply concerned about our personalities. He has called us to be His people in order to remold us in His own image, and then send us into life as liberated personalities. What He does for us is in preparation for what He wants to do through us in the world.

The parable of the leaven is the parable of the transformation of personality and, subsequently, the transforming power of a Christ-centered personality. It dramatizes how the Kingdom of God changes us and then how we, as changed people, affect the world. Jesus tells us how the gospel gets into us and then, how we are to get the gospel into the world.

The adventure of working with people is maximized for

me because I can share the pilgrimage of personality transformation with them. The most exciting times of my life are when I can be part of the Lord's implantation of the leaven in people. It's a delight to watch people change and grow after they have entered the Kingdom and allowed the reign and rule of Christ to be the leaven in their personalities.

The other day, I read a grim commentary on human nature: "If a man is a philanderer, he will always be a philanderer to the end. It is only in novels that a miracle occurs in the last chapter that makes the drunkard reform and become sober, the grouch sunny and sweet-tempered, the miser generous and open-handed, the shrew so mild that butter wouldn't melt in her mouth. In real life these things never happen. People continue to be what habit and usage have made them."

I don't believe that! Everything in my own experience and observation of people in whom the leaven of the Lord is at work convinces me that personality can be changed.

What Christ has been in us as the leaven, we are to be in the world. Once we have been leavened, we are to be the leavening agent of the Kingdom of God in the world. We are kneaded into the dough of society by our Lord. Our influence in the lives of others is like Christ's influence in us: pervasive, penetrating, and permeating.

Observe how Christ-centered personality becomes His leaven in the world. As the leaven pervades each aspect of our inner person, the result is manifested for others to see. We should be the source of repeated questions: How did you get the way you are? How can I find what you have found?

Our personality is our window to the world. People will be able to see what can happen to them by observation of what is happening to us. Leaven is observable only as it's working, not after the bread is baked. Our task is not to become "perfect," but to expose the leaven as it's working in us. As we share what the Lord is doing as well as what He's done, we will make contact with other struggling persons. Vulnerability and openness create contagious communication about the adventure of the Spirit's transforming work.

The test of a leavened personality is the number of people with whom we have been able to share our faith. Any Christian who is allowing the leaven to work in him will be besieged by people who also want to discover the dynamic.

I rely on you, Changeless God, to affect the metamorphosis in me which will captivate others with whom I share the Source of my difference.

SOARING TO THE UPSIDE OF LIFE

Since, then, you have been raised with Christ, . . . Set your minds on things above, not on earthly things. Colossians 3:1, 2, NIV

———◆———

The victory of Christ's resurrection enables the Christian to live a victorious life. The hope of the Resurrection is inseparably related to the promise of regeneration. For resurrection living, there is resurrection power.

"You have been raised with Christ." We need to think about what that means. Unification with Christ in His death and resurrection is the key to unlock the power of the victorious life. When we can surrender our lives to Christ we are incorporated into His dying and rising. To be committed to Christ is to die to ourselves and our control of our lives.

We are no longer in charge of our destiny. The self becomes the container and transmitter of the living Christ. When He comes to live in us, we experience a resurrection to a new level of living under His guidance and by His power. Pascal said, "It is one of the greatest principles of Christianity that that which happened in Jesus Christ may happen in the soul of the Christian. We have a linking not only with Calvary, but with His resurrection."

The victorious life flows from this exciting realization. Dedication to Christ begins a whole new life. Heaven, a vital union with Christ, begins. We have a new set of desires, a new purpose and a new perspective. That's what Paul means when he says: "You have been raised with Christ; set your hearts on things above." Heaven in our hearts is the vitality of the victorious life.

Paul knew that we become what we think about; we are inadvertently molded by the passions of our hearts. Our goals shape our priorities. Obviously, the Colossians had accepted Christ and His salvation, but their minds and hearts were still engrossed in "earthly things."

We can empathize. Long after we have begun the new life our thoughts, energy and time can be focused on our agenda of personal success and prosperity. This duality of direction is what debilitates so many of us. Saint Augustine said, "Christ is not valued at all, unless he is valued above all." That statement bruises our both/and mentality.

When many of us came to Christ we brought along our personal set of purposes, plans and priorities. To some He became little more than an addendum to a satisfied, settled life. After commitment to Him we continued life much as it had been before: the same convictions about life, the same desires, the same attitudes. No wonder we blend so comfortably into the secular scene. Our spiritual focus is on the things above; our verve and vitality is invested on things below. Paul called for a radical transformation of attention and a reordering of values.

To seek the things that are above in our obligations and responsibilities in the things on earth is the challenge of Christian living. That means recognizing that all things on earth belong to our Lord. As participants in the Kingdom of God, we are to seek His rule and authority in our daily living. The more we focus our minds on Him, the more we will be able to use earthly things to His glory. What we can taste, touch and tabulate can never be our satisfaction. Position, popularity and the people of our lives are not our security. But when they are, we become vulnerable candidates for discouragement and disappointment. Most of the things which upset us are the denial of desires which don't ultimately count.

The Christian can be victorious in life's difficulties because he can see them as transitory and absolutely incapable of separating him from his heavenly purpose. That's why Paul could say, "I consider that our present sufferings are not worth comparing with the glory that will be revealed in us . . . . .Who shall separate us from the love of Christ? Shall trouble or hardship or persecution or famine or nakedness or danger or sword? . . . No, in all these things we are more than conquerors through him who loved us. For I am convinced that neither death nor life, neither angels nor demons, neither the present nor the future, nor any powers, neither height nor depth, nor anything else in all creation, will be able to separate us from the love of God that is in Christ Jesus our Lord" (Rom. 8:18,35,37-39, *NIV*).

A woman once came to Ralph Waldo Emerson and said that the world was coming to an end. To that Emerson replied, "That's all right, I can get along without it." And so can we! The realization frees us to live with joy and delight. We can creatively love only what we do not need.

One of America's most famous and popular movie actors expressed to me the essence of the victorious life: "I never believed that either my talents or opportunities were anything but a gift. God gave them to me and I have used them for His glory. Disappointments, and what some people call frustrations, were only transitions so that I could see a new direction. If I hold fast to my conviction that Christ is in charge and knows what He's doing with me, how can I doubt His loving reordering of my life? When I surrendered having to succeed, I could handle success." Exactly! This man has broken through to freedom.

———————————◆———————————

Lord, help me keep my spiritual trajectory high-locked in on heavenly values. I want to be so detached from the world that I can love its occupants into the eternal kingdom of your Son.

KEEP YOUR SOUL-FIRE BURNING

Do not put out the Spirit's fire.
1 Thessalonians 5:19, *NIV*

Recently, in preparation for a conference in a church in the Midwest, I asked the church officers to write out their deepest hope for themselves and their church. The response of the elders, deacons and trustees of this prominent church all said the same thing in different ways. Their hope for themselves was that they could find the excitement of the new life in Christ and that their church would be filled anew with warmth and joy.

I hear the same longing from clergy at conferences wanting to find ways to renewing the local congregation. "How can we set our people on fire for Christ?" the pastors ask. "What can we do to recover the ebullient joy of New Testament Christianity in our time? Is there some program, some technique, a strategy we're missing?"

Before the conferences go very far we are usually up against the reality that something must happen to us before it can happen to our congregations. The need is universal among clergy, church officers and millions of church people. The fire has gone out, the enthusiasm has gone dull, boredom with churchmanship has set in.

Why? How can so many good Christians feel the way they do with what they believe? How did they get that way? What banked the fires for a long hiatus of mediocrity? Is it the exhaustion from endless committee meetings, lifeless worship services and irrelevant preaching?

I think I have discovered an answer. We have divided faith from life. It's possible to believe in Christ, be a participant in church activities and support fine causes and still miss the most obvious. The immediacy of the Lord is impinging on every situation. Intimacy with Him is discovered in opening all of life to Him and being amazed at what He can do with the people and problems of life.

We have arrived at a strange state of self-sufficiency in contemporary Christianity. We have organized out the possibility of Christ's surprising intervention. Our churches are filled with humanly adequate people who can handle daily living rather effectively. Prayer for Christ's power is reserved for big crises and monumental tasks.

In our churches, we talk about grand ideas of salvation, faith and grace. We seldom see the implications for marriage, the family, the loneliness of being single, the pressures on the job, difficult people and knotty complexities. Christ is off dealing with world problems; we should be mature enough to handle the rest. But most serious of all, we don't catch the momentous power available to maximize the mundane and sensitive life with the presence of Christ. Separating our living from our relationship with Christ eventually results in a bland and boring Christianity.

The way back to an exciting Christian life is to live in momentary companionship with Christ, surrender all of our relationships and responsibilities to Him as we go through the days, and discover the missed potential every person and problem has to offer. Christ is the mighty maximizer. He can take every hour and energize it with unexpected, unforeseen, uncalculated happenings. The joy comes from seeing Him at work. When we begin to share this truth with one another, there'll be a change in our churches. Our experience of the Savior will be updated daily and hourly with evidences of His power.

Sometimes my lazy faith smolders, Lord, annoying people with its fumes more than attracting them with its warmth. I welcome the Spirit's spark to set me ablaze with the excitement of following you with obedient abandon.

I'M FREE AT LAST!

So if the Son sets you free, you will be free indeed. John 8:36, *NIV*

I have spent over 40 years of my life in Christ seeking to be a free person. I long to be free to love, forgive, respond to life spontaneously, expect miracles and live as a celebrant of life. My experience of Christ's love constantly frees me from self-justification and guilt. His grace has liberated me to trust Him with my problems and needs. Countless interventions have convinced me that He knows my needs and will answer prayer beyond my fondest imagination. Times of self-doubt have been replaced by a deep inner peace. And yet, I have felt that I have only begun to experience what it means to be free.

The question of authentic freedom is not what can the Lord do to set us free, but what can we do to free up our lives for Him. That question forces us to wonder where in our lives we are tripping His glorious race. What areas have we kept back; what relationships of our lives are closed to Him?

The Lord frees us so we can give Him freedom. Authentic freedom is clearing the track, opening the way, removing the impediments, letting go with joyous abandonment.

The Christian life begins when we are released from the prisons of our own making. The love of the cross unlocks the prison doors of memory. The past is forgiven and the future is open to new possibilities. We are liberated to accept and love ourselves as loved by the Lord. This unshackles our relationships. We become natural, affirming people who care. Life loses its drudgery. Motivated by love, we want to serve the Lord.

All this is in preparation for the sublime freedom for which we were created. Now we are confronted with a new purpose for living. It's one stage of growth to say with Paul, "For to me to live is Christ" [Phil. 1:21, *KJV*) and quite another to say, "Christ in [me], the hope of glory" (Col. 1:27, *KJV*). Christ does not ask, "What have you done for me lately," but "What will you allow me to do in and through you today?" Our challenge is not to work harder for the Lord, but to give Him freedom to work.

———————◇═══╪═══◇═══◇———————

Lord, make me willing to be made willing! Heal my fears, unleash my timidity, unloose my clutching control.

GOD HAS PROGRAMMED YOU FOR PROGRESS

*Therefore, if anyone is in Christ, he is a
new creation; old things have passed away;
behold, all things have become new.*
2 Corinthians 5:17, *NKJV*

The other day, as I was driving along in my car, my attention was arrested by a billboard. In bold, black letters it said, "Prayer changes things!" I thought a lot about that as I drove along. Does prayer change things? Well, yes and no. Certainly, when we pray God does intervene and make a difference in circumstances. But at the center of most of the difficulties and problems we face are people. Usually the way God changes things is to change those people. And yet, one of the greatest miracles of prayer is how God changes us and then frees us to cooperate with Him in changing people. Wonderful things begin to happen when, through prayer, we allow Him to change our attitudes toward the people and problems we face.

I want to communicate an astounding promise. *We don't have to remain as we are.* We have been programmed for progress. William James said, "The most exciting discovery of our generation is that we can alter our person by altering our attitudes." Prayer is how it happens. There is a transforming power in prayer. George Bernard Shaw said, "Those who cannot change their minds cannot change anything." Prayer can be a mighty force in changing our minds about the people for whom we are concerned or distressed.

Look at it this way. When we have problems which are hassling our peace of mind, as we have said, the Lord instigates in us a desire to pray. We tell Him all about the problem and ask for His guidance. Or we are troubled about some person: a loved one who is in need, a friend whose life-style disturbs us, a fellow worker who doesn't measure up or a neighbor who upsets us by the way he or she lives.

Again the Lord is the initiator of the desire to pray about these people. Often we think that because we pray we can dispatch the Lord to straighten out these people according to the detailed specifications we have outlined to Him. When the answer isn't immediate, we wonder if He's heard us.

Then a wonderful thing begins to happen. Our attitude of worry, judgment, impatience or defensiveness begins to change. We begin to feel differently about the people. We see them through the eyes of our Lord. We feel love, understanding and compassion. Often it is our changed attitude which gives them the desire to change.

But even if they remain the same, we are able to cope much more effectively because of the transformation of our attitudes. We can't change most situations or people, until the Lord changes us. Changed people change situations around them. Beginning with them.

Have you ever thought of prayer as the dynamic communion with the Lord in which He seeks to transform you into His likeness? If so, are you presently yielding who you are to His healing and reformation? Have you ever asked Him to show you your full potential as His person? Do you dare to yield to His molding Spirit the future development of your personality?

"Therefore, if anyone is in Christ, he is a new creation; old things have passed away; behold, all things have become new" (2 Cor. 5:17, *NKJV*). And for what purpose? To love as we've been loved! Prayer doesn't just change things. It changes us.

Lord, what a change within us one short hour
Spent in Thy presence will prevail to make!
What heavy burdens from our bosoms take,
What parched grounds refresh as with a shower!
We kneel, and all around us seems to lower;
We rise, and all the distant and the near;
Stands forth in sunny outline brave and clear;
We kneel, how weak! we rise, how full of power!
Why, therefore, should we do ourselves this wrong,

Or others, that we are not always strong,
That we are ever overborne with care,
That we should ever weak or heartless be,
Anxious or troubled, when with us is prayer,
And joy and strength and courage are ،with
Thee![2]

———————————◇—————————————

*Lord, I refuse to settle for sameness when the dynamic of
transforming prayer can change me and the stifling circumstances around me.*

FIRE UP YOUR SPIRITUAL SPONTANEITY

He will baptize you with the Holy Spirit and with fire. Matthew 3:11, *NIV*

What is the one word which would personify the kind of person you long to become?

Recently at a meeting on the Holy Spirit, I asked each of the participants to select a word which would articulate the quality of life he or she wanted to live. Throughout the remainder of the meeting we were to refer to each other by the dynamic description we had selected. I was not surprised that most people chose a word which was quite opposite their natural personalities. We claimed the promise that the Holy Spirit would enable us to be the persons we were meant to be. What do you suppose I chose for myself?

When I became a Christian, a profound personality transformation began. My experience of the Holy Spirit, the indwelling Christ, has continued to liberate me to be a free person—free to love myself and others unconditionally. Daily I must surrender my tendency to caution, reserve, and defensiveness. The Lord's gift to me is to help me be able to give myself away. To fall in love with people and involve myself with spendthrift abandon in their needs. I long to be a completely open, ready-for-anything kind of person. I don't want to resist life in any way. If there has been any progress toward this goal, it is because of the moment-by-moment renewal of the Lord's Spirit in me.

Therefore, the name I have selected for myself is the focus of the kind of person the Spirit has envisioned in my imagination. Spontaneous Lloyd!

I am convinced that an authentic sign that we have become the residence of the Holy Spirit is that we are spontaneous. My working definition of spontaneity is openness, freedom, expectancy, willingness to be surprised and affirmation of the many-splendored thing we call life. The basic meaning of the word means "that which is done freely, arising from inherent qualities." Its root is from "out of free will." True spontaneity is the result of surrendering our wills to the indwelling Spirit so that the inherent qualities by which we respond to life are His. There is an uncalculating, unaffected, unbound excitement in us when the Spirit is given complete freedom to express Himself through us. We become all-signals-go! people who respond to life's opportunities and challenges with immediacy and intensity. We were meant to be spontaneous!

God has so much more to reveal to us each day. So

often we miss the beauty around us and the serendipities offered us because of our fearful effort to defend, protect and preserve ourselves. As a man said, "I have spent all of my life saving myself for something—I don't know what—and have missed the wonderful delight of living while I'm alive." I have determined to do just the opposite. What about you?

The opposite of spontaneity is stagnation. The other day, I came across an alarming document entitled "The Seven Steps to Stagnation." I found more of myself and the institutional church than I wanted to in each of them. Stagnation is an inevitable result of thinking and saying the following:

1. We've never done it that way.
2. We're not ready for that.
3. We're doing all right without it.
4. We tried that once before.
5. It costs too much.
6. That's not our responsibility.
7. It just won't work.[3]

After reading this sevenfold diagnosis of resistance to the new, the innovative, and the different, I asked God to set me free from saying any of them or expressing them in my attitudes. I began to keep a record of the number of times I heard them from Christians. It was astounding! Often, the very people on whom we depend to model life as a great adventure make these steps the charter of their stagnation. That led me to search the Scriptures for the impetus of authentic, Holy Spirit-originated spontaneity. I wanted something more than the reckless irresponsibility some people claim is spontaneity. How could I become truly spontaneous as God had intended me to be?

I found the answer in Paul's admonitions to the Thessalonians (1 Thess. 5:16-22, *NKJV*). In bold contrast to the seven steps to stagnation, here are seven steps to spontaneity. Check the extent of your authentic spontaneity on the basis of this seven-way biblical test.

1. Rejoice always.
2. Pray without ceasing.
3. In everything give thanks;
   for this is the will of God in Christ Jesus for you.
4. Do not quench the Spirit.
5. Do not despise prophecies.
6. Test all things; hold fast to what is good.
7. Abstain from every form of evil.

Allow me to suggest a contemporary interpretation of these seven strides to spontaneous living. Then I want to share what each can mean in your life and mine for today's incredible opportunities.

1. Accept the gift of enthusiasm.
2. Welcome life expectantly.
3. Dare to be an open person.
4. Thank God for what He will do.
5. Consider the future as a friend.
6. Set courageous goals.
7. Overcome the negative each day by doing a specific, positive good.

Spontaneity is the result of the fire of the Holy Spirit in us. *The first step to spontaneous living is to feed that fire with complete trust.*

"Don't quench the fire!" Paul tells us. The implication of

the Greek is "don't develop a habit of quenching the Spirit." The word "quench," when used of fire, means to extinguish, to smother or stifle. Paul does not mean that we can diminish the Spirit of God, but we can extinguish the fire He builds in our hearts or in others. The only way fire can be extinguished is by something outside itself. The apostle is concerned about anything which hinders the free flow of the Spirit in us or in the Christian fellowship.

When the fires of the Holy Spirit are fueled by our willingness, there is an uncontainable enthusiasm for the gospel, our new life in Christ, people, and the wonder of life. Enthusiasm is the key to great living.

Authentic enthusiasm is a gift. It is not the result of human effort. Many of us have tried on our own strength to become enthusiastic people, only to find that we run out of steam. When our enthusiasm is motivated by people, circumstances, or possibilities we are easily disappointed and become negative. It's not easy to always be sunny, on top, full of excitement.

What then is the secret of a consistent flow of enthusiasm? The fire of the Holy Spirit! Genuine enthusiasm has its unquestionable origin in the indwelling blaze of the Spirit's living in us. Samuel Chadwick, British preacher (1860-1932), said, "Men ablaze are invincible." And I would add, irresistible—spontaneous.

———————————◇——◇———————————

Great Liberating God, I renounce the shackles of spiritual stagnation which sometimes impede my pilgrimage as a new creation. Hallelujah for the spontaneity of your Spirit in me!

GOD'S TRANSFORMING LOVE

He Enables
My Growth

*When we reflect on what God has done with the
mustard seed of our first trusting response to the
gospel, we can yield our troublesome affairs to Him.
He's growing a mustard tree out of you and me.
Be sure of that!*

FAITH UP TO YOUR FRUSTRATIONS

*If you have faith as small as a mustard seed,
you can say to this mountain, 'Move from
here to there' and it will move. Nothing will
be impossible for you."*
Matthew 17:20, *NIV*

I had a difficult time going to sleep in the hotel room in the East. My body was on California time. After I had prayed my prayers and read for hours, sleep eluded me. Finally I turned on the television set. Between the scenes of an old western movie, a 30-second spot appeared on the screen. It caught my attention. In bold letters was the message, "Before you give up, call 866-3242."

I was not about to give up on anything except getting some rest, but my interest was piqued. I dialed the number and found that it was a Christian crisis-intervention ministry. The woman's voice on the other end of the line spoke before I identified myself. "Before you give up, try Jesus! Can I be of any help?"

I thanked her and told her that I was a Californian whose only problem was sleeplessness. She laughed, and we had a good conversation about her ministry to people who are about ready to give up.

Afterward, I reflected on the many people I know who are hanging on by a thin thread, about to give up. I pictured them: people ready to give up on their marriage after years of trying; others tempted to give up hope for a friend or loved one; still others who feel that whatever they do to change things, it doesn't work.

Ever feel that way? We all feel it at times. The temptation to give up—on people, relationships, projects, hopes and dreams. Sometimes on ourselves.

Impatience breeds discouragement and births self-incrimination. It's then that we say, "If I only had more faith! Things would be different if I had enough faith to face life's excruciatingly slow process. My faith just isn't big enough!" As if everything depended on the size of our faith, we spiral subjectively into misguided musings about our own adequacy. The bad mood which results drains our energy and spreads to the people around us like a contagious disease.

One summer, I preached at the Church of the Lepers in Taipei, Taiwan. The work among these rejected people was begun by a great lady named Lillian Dickson. It's called the Mustard Seed Ministry. An infinitesimally small seed of trust has unleashed the infinite power of God. Lillian believed that God had called her to begin the work. She trusted Him completely. Money began coming in from all over the world. The work expanded. Now the results tower like a great mustard tree. She was tempted often to

84

give up. The Lord wanted to amaze the world with what He could do with a little lady who had a grain of faith. The glory is now given to Him. When I saw the healed bodies and the transformed personalities that have resulted, I was given new courage and hope.

Focus the people, problems, and responsibilities that cause you discouragement. The issue is not the size of your faith any more than the light switch is electricity. Our only task is to flip the switch.

Prayer is the sacred time for mustard seed planting. The Lord waits for us to pray, "Dear God, I am faced with problems too big for me. But I believe you are able. I trust you and want only what you have planned for me and the people I love. The worst thing that could happen would be for me to miss anything that you have arranged for my welfare."

What is true for our problems is also applicable for our growth in Christ. He begins with the smallest of mustard seed beginnings. Our faltering confession of belief in Him starts a recreative, regenerating process that never stops. We look back on that first prayer of commitment and are amazed at what the Lord has done with our character and personality.

When we reflect on what God has done with the mustard seed of our first trusting response to the gospel, we can yield our troublesome affairs to Him. He's growing a mustard tree out of you and me. Be sure of that!

Lord, I believe you can grow something substantial and useful out of the tiny seeds of what I am today. I yield to your plans for a bumper crop in me!

LET THE CHRIST-LIFE GROW ON YOU

*O Lord, you are our Father. We are the
clay, you are the potter; we are all the work
of your hand. Isaiah 64:8, NIV*

───────────◆───────────

For God's sake grow up!" These sharp words of challenge were given to a man whose faith had not penetrated into his character and relationships. His commitment to Christ had remained a sentimental, infantile evasion and equivocation. He was not childlike, but childish. All of his attitudes and values were the same as he had before accepting Christ. Immobilized on dead center, he resisted growth at every turn. The troublesome flaws in his character remained unhealed. He needed to grow up—in Christ.

A commitment to Christ as Savior and Lord is a commitment to grow. The Lord is never finished with us. The more we discover of ourselves, the more we have to give to Christ's control. The more we discover of Christ, the deeper we grow in our relationship with Him. Every day demands honest facing of ourselves and areas in which we need His transformation. Prayer, Bible study, sensitivity to the Lord's presence and penetrating reformation—all result in the realization of the need for further growth. We have been called to be distinctly different!

The other day I was shocked to realize a need to grow in an area of my own life. Without knowing it, I had fallen into a manipulative pattern of grandstanding benevolence with my family. I had arranged some very fine opportunities of travel and announced them in a way that demanded approbation. What insecurity had prompted that? My wife alerted me, in as kind a way as she could, to how I was coming across. Suddenly, I was aware of an old pattern of relating to people I love. A prolonged time with my Lord exposed the trouble. For some reason an old insecurity had reared its ugly head. I had done the right thing for the wrong reason. Rather than doing the right thing out of love, I had done it to assure the flow of affirmation.

The interesting thing about this unsettling realization of the need to grow was that it had been preceded by a period of delicious satisfaction over my growth in Christ. I was thankful for all that the Lord was doing in my life and delighted by the progress we were making together. And then this disturbing realization of a new need to grow. Once again I experienced a truth I know, but often forget: the Lord is the potter and I am the clay; He has begun to mold me into His own image and He will be refashioning me all through my life. Every period of gratitude over what He's accomplished with me will be followed by an exposure of a new need to grow.

We all bring an old nature into the Christian life. The new creation in Christ is both immediate and gradual. When we surrender our lives to Christ, accepting Him as our Savior and Lord, we are ushered into a dynamic relationship. The moment we say yes! to Him we are assured of eternal life, His presence, and a never ending growth in His likeness. Our eternal destiny is no longer in question but our character is always in process. The Christian life is a never-ending growth in depth.

The reason for this is that becoming a new creation in Christ is a thorough, ongoing character reorientation. We have been conditioned by the religious, cultural, and social values of our time. Attitudes, reactions, goals and thought patterns have been inadvertently ingrained into the fiber of our natures. When we become Christians everything is suddenly exposed to Christ's scrutinizing renovation. Life as we have lived it is consistently exposed to a startling comparison with life as the Lord meant it to be. We can appreciate what's happening to us by observation of what the Lord longs to do in the lives of others.

Think of how disturbed we are by the behavior of some Christians. We become indignant when a person who professes to be "in Christ" does or says something which boldly contradicts his or her faith. Then after our flush of righteous indignation, finger-pointing, and lip-smacking judgmentalism, the Lord turns His searchlight of truth and honesty on us. "What about the contradictions in your own life? What if people knew about your inner thoughts, fantasies, distortions and selfish attitudes?" Suddenly our judgments are replaced by empathy. Given the same temptations or pressures, we may not have been any better. We are all unfinished and need to invoke the Lord's forgiveness on our "selfish strife" even as we pray and sing, "Finish then Thy new creation."[1]

Focus the areas where you need to grow in the new life in Christ. If He were to diagnose your next steps, what would He prescribe? Recently in a Covenant Bible Study group in which my wife and I are participants, each of us was challenged to write out a prescription he or she felt the Lord would write. It was enlightening to hear what each wrote. Though many in the group are seasoned saints who have lived the Christian life for years, all of us knew that we had barely begun. The Lord is up to a magnificent thing in all of us. We all needed affirmation of the progress He had made with us and a clear delineation of the next steps in being distinctly different people.

Master Potter, I know you are fashioning me into a vessel which is more useful with each spin of the wheel and touch of your creative hand. Thank you for your patient investment in my growth.

HOW TO
BE READY
FOR
ANYTHING

*Be on your guard; stand firm in the faith; be
men of courage; be strong.*
1 Corinthians 16:13, *NIV*

There's a chicory coffee concentrate from Scotland
that provides a delightful bit of memory of my student days in Edinburgh. On the label is a picture of a
kilted Scots regiment guard. The motto of the regiment is
printed above the imposing, armed, prepared-for-battle
highlander. "Ready, Aye, Ready!"

Not a bad motto for the beginning of a day. It usually
sparks some interesting breakfast conversation at our
house about the challenges of the day ahead. Often, when

my wife asks me how I am and what's anticipated in the day before me, I put on a thick, studied Scottish burr and chant with gusto, "Ready, aye, ready!"

I would really like to mean that for every day and all of life. I'd love to be the kind of person who's ready for anything. Each day brings its unanticipated opportunities, serendipities and problems. I want to live to the hilt in each of them.

That's not possible unless we expect and hopefully anticipate meeting the Lord in each new day. He gives the day and He will show the way. Disappointments become appointments for Him to give new direction. Difficult people are gifts for new dependence on the Lord for what He will give to meet the trying relationships of life. Perplexities are the prelude to receiving new power from the resourceful Lord. He comes each day with the gift of joy.

Robert Louis Stevenson was right: "To miss the joy is to miss all." Joy is so much more than happiness. It is the result of the experience of grace—God's unmerited favor and changeless love. I am convinced that there's reason for joy in all the delights and difficulties of life.

Joy springs forth whenever we experience the intervention of the Lord, maximizing the triumphs and tragedies of life. He brings good out of difficulties and multiplies our pleasures into blessings. He wants us to look for Him to invade the events of each day; to put joy in the joyless drudgery of life. We don't know what any day will bring. To be "ready, aye, ready" for life's surprises is demanding. It means being in good spiritual condition, with our prayer muscles well exercised.

I have a friend who precedes any significant statement she makes with, "Are you ready for this?" The question is a good one. How ready are we for what will happen to us and around us? So often I have heard people say, "I just was not ready for that! I was all set for the worst that could happen. I was caught off guard. I never expected something good to happen!" The lack of preparedness can minimize the truly creative experiences of life. We can become so negative that we expect the worst and are almost disappointed if it doesn't happen.

Our Lord wants a prepared and expectant people. Ready to be "surprised by joy" as C.S. Lewis expressed it. Christ has called us to be adventurers who have trusted the future to Him and anticipate His interventions in the most unexpected places and situations.

The oil of the Holy Spirit, the indwelling Christ, prepares us with expectancy and anticipation for the breakthrough of the Lord in each day's experiences. The old folk tune articulates the appropriate prayer in the light of that. "Give me oil in my lamp, keep me burning. Give me oil in my lamp, I pray. Keep me burning till the break of day." Then, in joyous anticipation of the Lord's coming, the song concludes with "Sing Hosannah to the King." Yes, to desire oil in our lamps results in the expectant desire of His coming again. "Sing Hosannah to the King."[2]

The Christians I know who have been filled with the oil of the Holy Spirit are bright and radiant Christians. They want the Lord, long for His interventions, expect them and are ready for them in the complexities and confusion of life. They are constantly on the lookout. What is the Lord saying to me in this? What is He trying to teach me in this problem? How will He come into this opportunity and enable me to grasp its full potential?

Being filled with the Holy Spirit makes us ready-for-anything Christians. We can say, "Let life happen! Let it come with winter winds and its disappointments; its springtime of unanticipated delight; its arduous days and restless nights. We are ready! We are open to grow, agile to regroup, free to fail, willing to cut our losses and able to surge ahead."

———————————◇———◆———◇———————————

As the One who knows the future, Lord, you can equip me for the eventualities of the day-by-day present. I anchor my readiness in your eternally contemporary sufficiency.

HOW TO
ENJOY
GROWING
PAINS

Rejoice always.
1 Thessalonians 5:16, *NASB*

R ejoice always. That, for me, means to welcome life
with expectancy. We can tackle all that life offers if
we can praise God for what happens to and around
us. The delight and the difficult; the routine and the seren-
dipitous. The key to unlocking both the challenge and the
concern of life is to rejoice with enthusiasm. This is not
simplistic sentimentalism. It is rooted in a profound trust
that God can use everything. We will discover new truth
and advance through life's pleasant and painful experiences. When disappointment or setbacks hit us they all
contain a hidden joy. We can wade into impossibilities with

enthusiasm because we have learned that our most pressing problems in the past have forced us to learn two essential lessons from life: (1) God is in charge; and (2) we have grown most when we've trusted Him in spite of difficulties.

Rejoicing enables us to embrace the ups and downs of life without reservation. When we expect to discover truth and growth from each person or circumstance, we are not disappointed.

While I was studying this passage, I had an experience which brought home the truth of "rejoice always." I had spent an entire day dictating responses to letters on my dictating machine. Each letter was composed with utmost care. Our church's television ministry has multiplied my correspondence and I try to be faithful in personally acknowledging prayer requests sent to me and gifts for the ministry. The tape was full of such communications.

After I finished, I put the tape in a folder to take to my office to give to my administrative assistant for typing and sending. Somewhere between the place where I had hidden away to get caught up on my mail and my office, the tape was lost! I was frantic to find it because of all the work. Hours of searching were unrewarded. Then it hit me: could I rejoice? Not easily. But following the advice I'd been writing in this chapter, I dared to rejoice that some good could come out of this goof.

A day later I realized that a couple of the letters I had dictated were far from maximum responses to the needs addressed to me. I was able to do them over. But the significant thing was that rejoicing gave me release from the tension of the foolish loss of the tape.

We all face trivial and momentous difficulties which will either destroy our effectiveness or enable us to let go of the frustration and pick up the broken pieces and start again. That can happen only if we rejoice that God can use everything for our growth and His glory.

I know a man who keeps a journal of each day's discoveries. At the end of each day, he writes down what God has taught him. He believes it's not the number of breaths we breathe but the number of breath-taking experiences each day offers. After a long period of resisting life, he has been liberated to expect the miracles of God in his daily life. He doesn't want to forget any of them. That's the reason he writes them down daily: he wants to be fortified to begin the next day with spontaneity.

The only way to take this crucial step to spontaneous living is to try it. Make this week a seven-day experiment. Resolve to rejoice! Not regardless of what comes your way, but because of it. There's a blessing waiting, wrapped up in each questionable eventuality. Expect it. Look for it. Thank God for it in advance. You will note the change that happens in your attitudes.

———————◦———————

Even in the humdrum monotone of life's drudgery, I hear the delightful song of joy, Lord, which calls me beyond grumbling to praise and rejoicing. Joy to the world, the Lord is come!

GROWING INTO NONSTOP PRAYER

Pray continually.
1 Thessalonians 5:17, *NIV*

A man came to see me about how to handle the mounting pressure in his life. I knew he believed in God, so I asked him to tell me about his prayer life. He told me that he had decided years ago to spend a period each morning in prayer and Bible study. "It just doesn't last through the day!" he said. "And things are so harried at work that there's no time to get away from it all to pray."

"Why not pray your way through the day right on the job?" I responded. He said he didn't think that would be possible with people around him all the time. Then I described the secret of prayer without ceasing and how to retreat into the living center of his own soul sanctuary.

"You think with people around, don't you?" I asked.

"I'd better," he laughed, "or I'd lose my job!"

"Then why not also pray?" I asked.

We talked about the power of brief arrows of prayer for wisdom, guidance, and help. I suggested that he send an arrow of prayer to God for the people, problems, and perplexities which were causing him tension. When things got tough, all he needed to do was claim that the Lord was present with him, that He was as concerned about carrying on a conversation with Him there at work as He was in the quiet early morning hours when he had his devotions.

"Think of it this way," I suggested. "One hundred ten and a fourth hours make one weak. Spell week, w-e-a-k."

"What do you mean?" the man asked, his interest piqued.

"Well," I said, "you have 168 hours at your disposal every week—seven times 24, right?"

He agreed to the obvious, with a smile.

"You sleep about eight hours a night," I continued, "so subtract 56 from that and you have 112 left. Now you tell me you spend about 15 minutes in prayer every morning—that's 1¾ hours each week. Subtract that and you have 110¼ hours left uninspired by communion with the Lord and unprotected by His guidance and care. No wonder you're living under pressure," I said urgently. "The hours at work where you're in the bind of impossible schedules and difficult people are unclaimed for the Lord."

I explained that Christ is the Lord of all life, that for Him there is no division between the sacred and the secular. In fact the word "secular" comes from the Latin root *saecularis,* meaning "of the now, belonging to this age." Every "now" moment is sacred to the Lord. His wisdom can be given for our thinking about problems and opportunities, and His guidance is available for our moment-by-moment decisions.

Then we talked about how to pray for each person as we talk to them or deal with them. In each problem-solving challenge we can pray, "Lord, I live with the results of so many poor decisions and wrong choices. Help me right now to think clearly and see all the facts of this complication. Show me what to be, do, and say."

The man's face brightened. He got the picture of living in the flow of supernatural power all through the unclaimed 110¼ hours at work, at home, at church, and in the community that had not been filled with the power of prayer. His response expressed excitement and the desire to experiment with praying all through the day. So I continued about prayer at night.

"And here's a way to clam those 56 night hours. Go to sleep praying. Ask the Lord to work in your mind all through the night and He will. You'll awake refreshed and have ideas and solutions that the day hours will demand."

"What a wonderful way to live!" my friend exclaimed.

"The only way to live adventuresomely and abundantly," I rejoined.

Marcus Aurelius once said, "The soul is dyed with the color of its leisure thoughts." I'd say that the soul is dyed with the color of our momentary thoughts all through the day.

The author of Proverbs was right when he stated that we are what we think in our hearts (see Prov. 23:7). We become what we think about all the time and if the Lord is given access to our thoughts in only a brief time of prayer each day, we will become less than the persons He intends us to be.

J.M. Barrie said, "To have faith is to have wings."

99

Wings of prayer lift us above the present pressures so we can get perspective and receive power to be maximum for the Lord.

Wherever I go, people tell me that their greatest problem is living out their faith in the daily round of activities and challenges. So often they express the desire to get away from it all to rediscover their relationship with the Lord. Now I'm a firm believer in retreats for spiritual renewal and times away alone for prayer and planning. But these times can only strengthen us to discover the resources of prayer for the daily demands of living. It's what happens to us in the battle which shapes our lives.

Lord, I never want my "prayer life" to interfere with our moment by moment prayer atmosphere and conversation. I relish the prospect of growing as a continual pray-er.

GOD'S GOODNESS IS MY GOAL

Examine everything carefully; hold fast to that which is good; abstain from every form of evil. 1 Thessalonians 5:21,22, *NASB*

I believe in ten-year, five-year, three-year, one-year and one-month goals. I can respond to or reject opportunities on the basis of my one-month goals in the light of my short- and long-range goals. The reason many of us get frustrated and lose our spontaneity is because we don't know where we are going. True freedom is always expressed within carefully defined limits. No great literature or art was every produced by a person who worked when he felt like it. No profound romantic love has been expressed to several among many. Choices must be made. Creativity is concentrated power from the Holy Spirit.

I know a man who takes a 72-hour period every year to be absolutely alone with God. The first 24 hours are spent getting thoroughly quiet. He cleanses his soul with forgiveness and grace. His mind is centered on God and all that He has been and done. The next 24 hours are spent envisioning where God wants him to be in 10 years. What are the Lord's goals and priorities? He writes them down carefully as prayer releases the flow. The gift of imagination focuses the image. He actually lives out in his mind the vision of 10 years hence. The last 24 hours are spent writing an "action description" of the steps to be taken in each of the 12 months of the year ahead. My friend leaves his retreat refreshed and determined. He knows what to say yes to and when to say no! He is spontaneous.

At the beginning of each month, he writes out what he must do in those 30 days to move forward to his one-year goals in the context of his ten-year plan. I had often wondered why he was so free of pressure. When he told me how he learned to envision the Lord's will for his life, I found the secret of his effectiveness.

We all need a basis of testing all things and holding fast to what is good. The word for "good" in Paul's admonition is *kalon* from *kalos,* meaning noble, beautiful, winsome, and attractive. There are two words for "good" in Greek. The other is *agathos* which simply defines a thing is good in quality. Kalos is so much more. Goodness is an attribute of God. It defines His consistency and faithfulness to His nature of pure love. He can be depended on to be true to His revealed nature of unfailing grace revealed in Jesus Christ.

In that light, the good is that which is consistent with God's plan and purpose for us in Christ. We have an irreducible maximum for our primary goals. What will help us grow to the measure of the stature of the fullness of

.Christ? What will make us more like Him in word, action, attitude, and spirit? What will further the Kingdom in our lives—that is, His reign and rule? Once we answer these questions we can move on to secondary goals. What particular task has He called us to do? Where will we be in 10 years in accomplishing the specific thing each of us, and no other, was born to do? Both the primary and secondary goals are part of the "good" for us. We are called to be unique miracles of our Lord.

There are few things which give life more verve than knowing "what is that good and acceptable and perfect will of God" (Rom. 12:2, *NKJV*) in the short- and long-range goals of our lives. We know where we are headed and can react with spontaneity to everything which brings us closer to our destiny and destination as persons. And the Holy Spirit will guide us each step of the way!

Thank you, Almighty Father, that your plan for me is framed within your eternal plan for creation. I purpose only to set my personal goals within the context of your will for me.

MOVING FROM RULES-RELIGION TO RELATIONSHIP

You died with Christ to the basic principles of this world. Colossians 2:20, *NIV*

One of the most difficult challenges for Christians in every age is to remain in vital union with Christ in the midst of cultural religion. Every nation and community has its values, beliefs and practices which contradict the lordship of Christ and our absolute loyalty to Him. Christians have always been distinguished for daring to follow Christ and not the distorted, distracting cultural ideas of what life is supposed to be. The pressure to conform is often unbearable and painful.

104

To be free from the "oughts" of previous religious compulsions and conditioning is not easy. Long after we are set free in Christ, the old memory tapes are replayed with guilt-producing regularity.

I was raised in a church atmosphere where following Christ and remembering the things I should not do were blended into one admonition. Often the don'ts were all I heard. To be a Christian meant not being able to do many of the fun things most kids enjoyed. Also, there were obligations to being a Christian which were fragmented from union with Christ. I ended up with a list of demands with no dynamic to live them.

I became very hostile to man-made religion. Like the scribes of old, my religious instruction had a regulation for every situation spelled with two letters: no! Christ became a negation of the verve of life, the desire to grow intellectually and the delight of being alive. The judgmentalism of the advocates of the rules-religion drove me from the Christ they felt they wanted me to know.

Dependent and inseparable union with Christ is the only way any of us can know the difference between right and wrong, important and irrelevant. When we are united with Christ and through Him with one another in the Body, we can sort out creatively the implications of His lordship for our behavior, ethics and practices. God wants the Church to grow in maturity and power, not in slavish observance of regulations.

The death and resurrection cycle of the Christian life liberates us from past values and customs. We have died with Christ, and with that death all our old attitudes, compulsions and obligations died with Him. We have been raised by His power to a new life in Christ.

A radical healing takes place when we surrender our old selves to Christ and die to what's past. The tissues of the brain are reordered around the mind of Christ. The messages we send from our minds to our emotions and will are guided by Christ. The new creation is a miracle of the indwelling Christ.

I praise you, God, for freedom from the performance-oriented rules-religion treadmill and for the fresh newness of a daily relationship with you.

GOD AT WORK— PLEASE BE PATIENT!

The Kingdom of God is like a man who cast seed upon the ground; and goes to bed at night and gets up by day, and the seed sprouts up and grows—how, he himself does not know. Mark 4:26,27, NASB

If I could have the confidence in the midst of crises and challenges that I have after they are over, how much more abundant my life would be. I am much better at retrospective interpretation of what God has done than I am at relaxed insight about what He's doing.

After a storm has passed I can see what the Lord was doing in the tumult better than I can ride out the present storm. It's much easier for me to look back and observe the goodness of the Lord than to trust His graciousness in the fast currents of uncertainty and waiting. The area of my life where I need to grow is in patience in the process. I share this because I suspect there are many of you who identify with me in this. The process of God's evolving plan for us is as crucial as the product. But so much more difficult to endure.

I am alarmed at how little I remember of how God has worked in the past when I face difficulties in which I need the confidence that He is at work right now. How could I forget? But I do. Perhaps you suffer from impatience as much as I do.

Jesus planted the seed of the Kingdom of God in the soil of history. Over hill and dale in every heart that would listen, and then, on a bare hill called Calvary, He planted Himself. The world has never been the same: a band of disciples, a Spirit-filled church at Pentecost, a missionary movement to the reaches of the world, and now the only hope for our psycho-cybernetic creation. Two thousand years, but a moment in eternity beyond calculated time. Why does it take so long? We are chained to our conception of progress; bound by our lack of vision. God is working His purposes out. The seed is planted, the blade is piercing the hard crust of our resistance. We cannot stamp it out. It's growing. The kingdoms of this world are becoming the kingdoms of our Lord!

In that context, we can enjoy the persistence of God in us. When was the seed planted in you? It happened to me as a freshman in college. I heard the good news of God's love in Christ and had my imagination turpentined by a fellowship of Christians who gave me a picture of what God meant my life to be. I accepted Christ as my Saviour. Trusting Him as Lord of my life has not come as easily. Each new surrender of the facets and relationships of my life fertilizes the seed.

Allow your mind to drift back over what has happened to you since you first gave your life to Christ. Capture the memory of that moment. Next, allow your mind the luxury of relishing the times you knew God's intervention and inspiration. We can feel the growth of the seed of the reign and rule of God. We are not the people we were. Nor are we now what we shall be.

A couple of years ago my wife was seriously ill with cancer. Her own prayers about the future gave her a firm confidence that she would be well. She placed the seed of that God-given vision in the ground. Together we thanked God that what He told us would come true. The long period of surgeries, treatments and therapy seemed endless. The temptation to fear was ever-present. But God was faithful to His promise. His timing was not ours. Now she is well again, healed by the Holy Spirit.

As a spiritual leader, I have to put seeds of commitment into the ground constantly. God has given me an exciting vision for the local church in America. But repatterning the church around the mind of Christ takes time and patience. Whenever I get anxious, God reminds me of this parable. Plant the seed and leave its growth to Him!

As a parent, I have to relearn that repeatedly. God has given me three unique and special children. In each stage of their growth as persons, I have had to be reminded that they belong to the Lord. My memory verse as a parent is Philippians 1:6: "And I am sure that God who began the good work within you will keep right on . . . until his task within you is finally finished" (*TLB*). God is not finished with me or the people I love. The challenge is to trust that He always finishes what He starts. The future is in His hands!

Loving Father, I know I am not the person I was, but neither am I now what I shall be. Thank you for your persistent work in me and for the fruit of patience which helps me endure the growth process.

LORD, KEEP MY FAITH FRESH!

No one pours new wine into old wineskins. If he does, the new wine will burst the skins, the wine will run out and the wineskins will be ruined. No, new wine must be poured into new wineskins.
Luke 5:37,38, *NIV*

There's a great difference between the God of our experience and our experience of God. It's possible to become so dependent on our previous knowledge and understanding of God in our lives that we become closed to new discoveries and growth. We can reflect with gratitude on the ways God has worked in our lives in the past and miss the interventions of His love right now.

There are Christians who can recount with elaborate detail how they first discovered God's grace in some experience of need or challenge. Often the treasured memory

110

becomes more important than God Himself. His question is, "What have you allowed me to give you and do for you lately?"

A sure sign of a vital Christian is viability. He or she is open to grow and capable of freedom and flexibility. Faith is dynamic, not static. Fellowship with God is an adventure which is never completed. He wants us to be open and receptive to new truths about Him and fresh encounters with Him in our daily life. He is never finished with us and, therefore, we are never finished growing. Whatever has happened to us, it is only a prelude to what God is about to do. He is engaged in a momentous transformation in each of us. We have hardly begun to become the person He is ready and able to liberate us to be. There's never a time when we can settle into satisfaction or complacency. The Lord is on the move in you and me.

And yet, there is something in all of us which longs for the tragic tranquility of memories rather than forward movement. We resist the penetration of the Spirit of God into untouched areas of our personalities and habit patterns. We want to say, "Lord, I've learned enough for a while. Just allow me to enjoy life as it is without any crises or difficulties which force me to change and grow!"

Many of us have built a whole theology on our personal experiences of God. Soon our experiences build us. They become limitations to further development and expansion of our understanding. We become rigid and immobilized. We insist God must always do what He's done and be for us what He's been.

Life is filled with predictably unpredictable events. We can never freeze-frame God and be sure that we know all there is to know about Him. The moment we think we have captured all the "unsearchable riches" of his nature, He breaks out of our carefully fashioned mold. True, He is

111

"the same yesterday, today and tomorrow," but all that He is takes eternity to realize. A special joy is given to "What's next, Lord?" teachable saints. The unfolding drama of life is for the unveiling of aspects of His nature that we will never learn if we become comfortably settled on dead center.

I know this to be true for my life. When I am finished with my careful categories of how God deals with me and am sure that the best God has to give has been given, He forces me to face my spiritual immaturity by giving me an opportunity or problem which is so far beyond my strength that I am amazed that I could ever have been satisfied with my previous relationship with Him.

The God of my experience is constantly in competition with my fresh experience of God. But He will not allow me to break the first commandment and have other gods before Him—not even the idol of my dependence on the past. I have discovered that my tenacious hold on reflections of great experiences of the past is really fear of the future. The false security of the familiar must constantly be replaced by trusting God with the complexities and uncertainties staring me in the face today.

The parable of the new wine in old skins exposes the inadequacy of trust in our experience of God. It tells us that whatever we have known of God can be like an old, dried, cracking wineskin. The new wine of fresh experiences will burst the old skin.

The Lordship of Jesus Christ cannot be poured into the old skin of our settled personality structure, presuppositions about life, prejudices about people, plans for the future and predetermined ideas of what He will do or how we will respond. The dry, cracked bags of the past will burst; we will lose our cherished religion and Him as well.

Once the Lord takes up residence in us a dynamic process begins by which everything is made new. He reorders the tissues of our brains so that we can think His thoughts. Memories are healed and liberated. Values and purposes are reoriented. Our image of ourselves is transformed. He is satisfied with nothing less than molding us into His own image. The miracle of the new creation begins—and never stops. The old person in us is made into a new person. That's the inside story of conversion and sanctification. We become new creatures in Christ.

All this leads me to a personal decision I hope you will share. I have learned a great deal through study of Scripture and years of fellowship with the Lord. But I suspect that my most exciting years are ahead. How about you? If so, I want to surrender any false pride or dependence on the past and make a fresh beginning. My past experience of God can never substitute for the experience of God today.

Lord, here is a fresh wineskin; fill me. Here is my naked need; clothe me with your character. I can't wait to see what you will do!

GOD'S TRANSFORMING LOVE

He Inspires My Allegiance

God's conversations with us always get back to the same subject: the Kingdom of God, His rule and reign in our hearts. All of life's experiences are occasions for fresh communication about the next steps of His strategy in discovering, discerning and doing His will.

HELP FOR THE HEARING-IMPAIRED HEART

Give Thy servant an understanding heart.
1 Kings 3:9, *NASB*

The television interviewer asked me to prepare several questions I would be willing to answer on a talk show. They were to be questions which would explore aspects of my life as a speaker and writer. One of the questions I submitted caused no small alarm among the people preparing the script.

"What has God been saying to you these days?"

I intended the question to give me an opportunity to share fresh insights and visions my studies and observations of life had produced. The question sparked a reaction in the host of the program as well as the scriptwriters.

"What do you mean, 'God saying to you?' Does your God talk? When do you hear Him? How do you know it's

His voice? Do you claim some special pipeline to heaven?"

I did my best to clarify. No audible voice—an echo in my soul; fresh thought; insight and wisdom; convictions from ancient truth. But more than that, a communication from God comes as I read Scripture, take time for meditative prayer, listen to people, observe the Almighty's signature in nature, and live in-depth in life's challenges. God whispers in my delights, speaks in my problems, and shouts in my perplexities. He impinges on my every moment, waiting for me to listen to what He has to say. My most exciting times are when I pause in the midst of my studies and daily duties to ask, "Lord, what are you trying to say to me in this?" Suddenly what I'm reading or facing takes on new meaning. God breaks through. What He has to say is registered on my thoughts and feelings. He intends that His communication be expressed in my character and actions.

You and I are part of the sublime work of God's creation. He has created us with capacities to listen to Him. Jesus is His ultimate Word to us. In Him, God has spoken to us about what He wants to have happen to us, between us and through us in society. God's conversations with us always get back to the same subject: the Kingdom of God, His rule and reign in our hearts. All of life's experiences are occasions for fresh communication about the next steps of His strategy in discovering, discerning and doing His will. What He desires from us is what Jesus longed for as the response of the throngs of people who came to consider His message: a hearing heart.

Jesus is compassionately concerned about the hearing capacity of our hearts. He knows all about us: what life has done to us and what we've done to ourselves to impair the delicate listening ability we have been given. As we catch His eye, He gives us a knowing look. He understands the grids we have placed over our hearts and how little can get through. Does He know about our set ideas and inflexible presuppositions? Is He aware of our prejudices, our wardrobe of excuses, our resistance to truth? Yes! In His gaze we can't seem to hide our hurts which have made us unfeeling. He knows how out of touch we are with our feelings about ourselves and others. Most of all, He is aware of beliefs and convictions which have never been put into concrete actions of obedience. Jesus understands what's happened to our hearing hearts.

I have observed hardhearted Christians with hearing problems in churches across our land. They have set ideas and beliefs. Customs and familiar practices developed through the years take on the authority of the Ten Commandments. Political beliefs and economic theories are baptized with holy fervor. The Americanized Jesus of our own making makes it difficult to listen to the biblical Christ. Arnold Toynbee was right: familiarity is the opiate of the imagination. We develop familiar patterns of lifestyle, church life and priorities which become more important than Christ Himself!

But hardness of hearing is caused by an even deeper problem. Whenever we have a conviction we do not live out, we block our sensitivity to hear further truth. We are so constituted that the final step of hearing is action on what we heard. Ruskin said that every duty we omit obscures some truth we might have known. Every thought and emotion must have a creative expression. The great danger for us as church members is the immense truth and insight we are given each week in sermons, Bible study, and fellowship. If we do not express what's impressed we will get depressed.

Periodically in my church we take a small band of our members off for a spiritual retreat. We all go through an inventory of our hearing ability. It's like a medical checkup with a doctor. We probe to discover how open we are to listen to God. The greatest single cause of impaired hearing of fresh truth is the refusal to live what we know already.

At the end of one of these retreats, a prominent member said, "My Christian life has become dull and bland. I was no longer inspired or uplifted by worship or fellowship. Today, I found the reason. I hate to hear familiar truths and ideas I have refused to apply. I had closed my mind." We talked about a few basic things this man would dare to do in subsequent weeks. I saw him recently and was delighted to learn that his hearing had been restored. His eyes sparkled as he said, "I feel like I did when I first became a Christian. It's been like falling in love again!"

God is speaking to each of us right now as we read this. What does He have to say? He wants us to know how much He loves us. For our sins, He wants to give us Calvary's assurance. His perspective and power are offered for our possibilities and problems. He wants to reign supreme in our hearts so we can pray, "Thy Kingdom come. Thy will be done" (Matt. 6:10, *KJV*). The Lord is ready to guide the future. He offers insight, discernment and wisdom for the alternatives which face us. Most of all, He wants to give us Himself.

A hearing heart responds with sincerity. It is an honest and good heart. Not double-minded or seeking to serve two masters. It is a prayerful heart, holding fast what God has said, pondering it until it yields the gift of understanding. Listening to God takes time and attentive effort. It means spreading out all our concerns and cares before Him and saying, as Eli instructed Samuel, "Speak, Lord; for thy servant heareth" (see 1 Sam. 3:9, *KJV*). And speak He will! Each new communication is dependent on the enactment of a previous guidance. Fresh light is given if we walk in the light we have been given.

<hr>

Keep talking to me, Lord! By your grace I will not only hear but heed.

O COME, LET US ADORE HIM

Praise the Lord, O my soul; all my inmost being, praise his holy name.
Psalm 103:1, *NIV*

———————◇◇◇———————

Successful prayer is not measured by how much we get from God, but how much of Him gets into us and our daily circumstances and relationships. Prayer is not a "gimme game" but a grace lift. It is not being able to convince God of what we ought to have, but allowing Him to convince us of what we need and He is ready to give.

All great praying begins with adoration. God does not need our praise as much as we need to give it. Praise is like a thermostat that opens the heart to flow in communion with God. Hallowing God's name is enumerating His attributes. When we think magnificently about God's

122

nature we become open to experience afresh His glory in our lives.

I once took a course in creative conversation. The key thing I rediscovered was that there can be no deep exchange with another person until we have established the value of that person to us. Just as profound conversation with another person results from our communicating that person's worth to us, so too, we become receptive to what God wants to do in our lives when we have taken time to tell Him what He means to us. Don't hurry through adoration. Everything else depends on it. Tell God what He means to you, pour out your heart in unhurried moments of exultation. Allow Him to remind you of aspects of His nature you need to claim in the subsequent steps of prayer. Don't forget He is the leader of the conversation. The more we praise the Lord, the more we will be able to think His thoughts after Him throughout our prayer. He loosens the tissues of our brains to become channels of His Spirit.

Praise is the ultimate level of relinquishment. When we praise God for not only all He is but what He is doing in our lives, we reach a liberating stage of surrender. Often when we begin our prayers, we don't feel like adoration. Sometimes we wonder what God is doing with us in the difficulties and trials of life. Praising Him reestablishes the fact in our minds that He knows what He is doing and makes us receptive to His guidance in those very needs.

I've experienced that repeatedly. When I'm inundated with problems, my temptation is to rush past adoration to tell the Lord the particular thing I think He ought to do to help me. When I take time to reflect on the greatness of God in spite of my circumstances, I am much more ready to receive fresh wisdom when I pray about specifics.

A good way to recapture the power of praise is to read

the Psalms. I find a creative two-week adoration assurance is to read Psalms 95 through 108, one each day as a prelude to my own praise. They reestablish my trust in God's power, providence, and all-knowing love. My heart begins to sing again and then soar in communion with the Lord. The point is that God wants us to enjoy Him! He delights to bless us when we let go of our worries and fears in unfettered praise.

There are times when I've found it helpful to begin my prayers by saying, "I love you, Lord. Let me tell you why." Then I rehearse in my mind all that He's been for me. Soon He takes over and leads me in remembering His goodness and grace. In times of difficulty, dark moods are lifted, troubled spirits are transformed, and an unwilling heart is made receptive. Or in bright times of success and smooth sailing, my happiness is maximized into pure joy. But whatever the circumstances of life, adoration creates the sublime delight of being in the presence of the Lord. Worship in the ancient English means "worth-shape," or establishing the worth, the wonder, and the glory of God in our minds and hearts. Adoration is the beginning of powerful praying. God created us to receive and return His love.

I join in the adoration anthem of angels and redeemed humanity of every age: Praise the Lord! Praise the Lord! Praise the Lord!

THE THERAPY OF THANKSGIVING

*Give thanks in all circumstances, for this is
God's will for you in Christ Jesus.*
1 Thessalonians 5:18, *NIV*

———————————◆⊱◆⊰◆———————————

Thanksgiving is the key which unlocks our potential
and makes us receptive to more of the Lord's
power. Praise and adoration expressed in thanksgiving open the floodgates of the Spirit. The more we give
thanks, the more we can receive.

A person in Christ comes to learn that thanksgiving
not only gives praise for the pleasures of life but also for its
problems. Thanksgiving heals pride and opens the door to
the Lord's blessing in times of difficulty. When things are
going well and we give thanks, we acknowledge that all of
life is a gift; but more so in anguishing perplexity.

The very moment we can thank God for a problem, or
an impossible person or situation, we become open to

receive the help the Lord is ready to give. He can bless a thankful person whose heart is open and receptive.

A woman who has faced physical infirmities expressed the dynamics of thanksgiving to God: "I was resentful and hostile that this thing happened to me. I could see no reason for it. Then a friend helped me to thank God for what could happen in me through what was happening to me. My recovery began in that moment of gratitude. God had been ready long before to help and heal me. It was as if my thanksgiving was a final surrender and acceptance."

A man said the same thing about some difficulties in his marriage: "When I thanked God that He was at work in us in spite of our problems, I felt release and freedom. I know that the long process of reconciliation began when I could praise God—not that He sent the difficulty, but that He would use it to bring us to a new life together."

A young man facing uncertainties about the future was able to thank God for the valley of indecision.

A pastor thanked God for a tradition-bound church. His thanks broke him free to lead his people in freedom.

Recently, I was asked to contribute a list of my 10 favorite hymns to a compiler of a new hymnal. I submitted these as hymns which have sustained and strengthened me in so many times of need:

"Amazing Grace"
"Guide Me, O Thou Great Jehovah"
"Beneath the Cross of Jesus"
"Crown Him with Many Crowns"
"Joyful, Joyful, We Adore Thee"
"Praise Ye the Lord, the Almighty, The King of Creation"
"The Lord Is My Shepherd" (Crimmond)
"O for a Thousand Tongues to Sing"
"How Great Thou Art"

126

"Jesus, Jesus, There Is Something About That Name"
"Holy, Holy" (Jimmy Owens)
"To God Be the Glory, Great Things He Has Done"
"Because He Lives" (Gaither)

As I made up the list, I realized how much these hymns had meant to me in times of frustration. I can vividly remember how much William Cowper's hymn meant to me at a time of spiritual peril:

God moves in a mysterious way
His wonders to perform;
He plants His footsteps in the sea,
And rides upon the storm.
Deep in unfathomable mines
Of never-failing skill
He treasures up His bright designs,
And works His sovereign will.[1]

And many times at memorial services I have sung Luther's "A Mighty Fortress Is Our God" with families with whom I had shared the loss of a loved one. Hymns of trust and confidence unbind the frustrated or grieving heart to thank and praise God.

Karl Barth once said, "A church which has no great anguish on its heart will have no great music on its lips." The Psalter and the hymnbook are wonderful resources for daily devotions. Also, it's uplifting to take a portion of Scripture from the New Testament and sing its words with joy as the spontaneous music flows from a thankful heart.

Thank you, Lord, for today—its opportunities, complexities and difficulties. May you find a song of thanksgiving in my heart even before I see the results of your intervention in today's events.

COMMITMENT: YOUR DOORWAY TO GOD'S BEST

Commit your way to the Lord, trust also in Him, and He shall bring it to pass.
Psalm 37:5, *NKJV*

On the cross, Jesus repeated a prayer which every Hebrew child learned at his mother's knee. "Into Your hand I commit my spirit" (Ps. 31:5, *NKJV*). It is a good motto for our conversation with the Lord. The same releasing quality is expressed in Proverbs 16:3, "Commit your works to the Lord, and your thoughts will be established" (*NKJV*). All these Scriptures offer a great promise. Commitment leads to openness. We can discover the Lord's guidance in these challenges which have been turned over completely to Him.

Commitment is the missing ingredient of contempo-

128

rary Christianity and the reason so many miss the power of prayer. Many of us believe in the Lord, but have never made a commitment of our lives to Him. We are running our own lives. Prayer becomes a kind of magic to get God to do what we think is best for our lives. We break the first commandment: we have another god before the Lord— ourselves. When a crisis strikes we run to the Lord for help. It's usually to get His assistance to do what we've planned.

Too severe an analysis? How do you feel about that from your own experience of prayer? Ever sought God's help to accomplish plans that were never committed to Him or the result of His guidance?

When I talk with people who are experiencing a lack of power in their prayers or seldom sense the presence of the Lord, so often the cause is traced back to the absence of complete commitment.

I talked to a man recently who was facing difficulties with his daughter. Her life did not reflect his values or his beliefs. Tension and hostility sparked like electricity whenever they were together. The man prayed about his daughter's problems daily. There was no question in his mind what his daughter should do and be, and he told God repeatedly.

When he came to see me about what he called his "impossible problem," I felt led to ask him how he was praying about it. His response clearly indicated the real problem. He had never surrendered the need to the Lord, asking what He wanted him to be as a father and a communicator of affirmation and encouragement to his daughter's efforts to find out who she was and where she was going. He had to become a friend to establish the right to be heard. Imperious commands only caused greater rebellion. When he stopped telling the Lord what to do, and committed the broken relationship between him and his daughter, he began to see the quality of father she needed. He asked the Lord to show him the person he needed to be with her.

The result was that he began empathizing instead of criticizing. He not only was able to help her make some crucial decisions about her life, but discovered the secret of dynamic prayer. The only things which can ultimately hurt us and those we love are the things we refuse to commit to the Lord's wise and incisive guidance.

What are the problems and perplexities on your mind right now? In what areas are you clenching your fists and saying, "I've got to take care of this on my own"? Open those fists and put the needs into the trustworthy hands of our Lord. He is worthy of the trust. He's been handling people and problems for thousands of years. He is able.

You have won my heart, Lord, and I trust you implicitly. I release my selfish, fearful grip on my own life and affairs and commit them unreservedly to you.

DO WHAT
YOU
KNOW

I shall run the way of Thy commandments,
for Thou wilt enlarge my heart.
Psalm 119:32, *NASB*

Discovering and doing the will of God is the only way to have a consistent experience of the abundant life Jesus came to reveal and enable in us.

I want to reach out to you as I write and you read this. Empathy pulses within me. We all have decisions to make. The future looms with uncertainty. All of us are on the edge of some crucial evaluation of the next steps for our lives. What shall we do about the alternatives before us? How about the relationships that are demanding? How shall we act and what shall we do? In what way can we be maximum for God with the people we love? What does God want us to do in the complex problems that seem to defy solution?

Often we pray our prayers urgently seeking the Lord's direction. We say, "Lord, show me your will!" Why is it so few people get a clear answer?

There is no question asked of me more often than this: "How can I know the will of God?" The question is a symptom of something much deeper.

Our family is blessed by the care of a very astute internist. He has a delightful way of asking incisive questions to get at the real reason causing the problem. When one goes to him with a headache, instead of giving a simple pain remedy, he plumbs the depths to find out the physical or emotional cause. He never deals with the symptomatic surface problem until he understands the reason.

In the same way, when someone says to me that he or she wants to know the will of God, I feel led by the Spirit of God to penetrate the inner reasons motivating the question.

Two basic assumptions guide my conversations with people about the will of God. The first is: If we are seeking to know the will of God, it's a sure sign that we are out of it. The second is: We cannot know the will of God unless we are willing to do the obvious, primary thing God has told us to do.

A friend of mine sits down at his desk each Monday morning and says, "This is the week! In everything I do this week, I am going to do the will of God." Then, he says, often before Monday morning is over he realizes that he has slipped back into self-dependence, cultural values and company policies which cannot stand the test of the Kingdom of God.

Before we are too critical of my friend, we need to

consider the ways we deny what we believe and what God has guided us to do. We see the issues and make bold protestations, but too often when we look back over a day we realize that we talked way beyond our action.

Have you ever had the feeling that God wanted you to do something and you avoided it? Ever feel the gnawing uneasiness that there are things He has made clear as action-steps and you resisted the guidance persistently? Not petulance; just neglect.

Religiously, I constantly promise God more than I produce. What about you? Most of us are great verbalizers who have the words without responsible obedience.

The discovery of the will of God comes from habitual, consistent, repetitive communion with God. If we say, "I don't know what the will of God is for my life," it means that day by day we've not been listening to the elementary guidance which results from faithful prayer and communion. When we seek God, not just His will, we will be ready for life's crises. The Lord seeks open, receptive disciples who are obedient to what they have been told in order that God may give them immediate guidance for each new challenge where the reality of the problem intersects with the resources of His Spirit. The only way to know the will of God for life's big decisions is to be willing to start today to be obedient in the little things.

The psalmist's prayer in Psalm 119:32 is the basis for daily obedience which opens future guidance. We need to read it often as a chart for life's treacherous seas. All through the psalm the author asks for strength to do the basics so the Lord can prepare for him His blessings. Our enlarged heart is open to new vision. In Psalm 86, David prayed the longing of all our hearts. "Teach me thy way, O Lord; I will walk in thy truth; unite my heart to fear thy name. I will praise thee, O Lord my God, with all my

133

heart, and I will glorify thy name for evermore" (Ps. 86:11,12, *KJV*).

If you were to ask me what my wife thinks or wants in a certain situation, I should not have to go to ask her. Over 35 years of marriage should give me some knowledge of her convictions, wants and desires. If I had to say, "Just a moment, I will ask her to hear what she has to say about that," it would say something about our marriage. To be sure, most women want some mystery about them, but if your question dealt with the basics of life, I should be able to tell you without a lengthy consultation with my Mary Jane. I have lived, talked and prayed with her through the years. I know my wife. Should we be less sure of God and His will?

Paul discovered that secret of knowing the will of God. "I urge you therefore, brethren, by the mercies of God (what He's done in Christ and has done repeatedly through Him in our needs), to present your bodies a living and holy sacrifice, acceptable to God, which is your spiritual service of worship. And do not be conformed to this world, but be transformed by the renewing of your mind (consistent, habitual prayer), that you may prove (test through experience) what the will of God is, that which is good and acceptable and perfect" (Rom. 12:1,2, *NASB*).

The Apostle had experienced what he wrote. He was a man under orders. Because He obeyed, the Lord unfolded more and more of His strategy to him. He challenged the church at Ephesus to do all things "as to the Lord." The Thessalonians were reminded of the basics. "This is the will of God, your sanctification" (1 Thess. 4:3, *NASB*). Growth in holiness as called, chosen saints would take place in following what the Lord had already made clear. Fresh direction would be given as a result of essential ethics for daily living. We cannot expect to know the will of

God if our lives are a rebellious contradiction to the message and life of the Master.

When our wills are obedient, the Lord will use all the faculties of our minds and emotions to impress on us what He wants us to do. He will use insight from others, confirmed in us by His Spirit, to point the way. But the final assurance will come in communion with Him. At the right moment, never too early or too late, we will know what to do or say. The answer will come from the voice of God within.

When it comes to knowing your will, Lord, I want to be very near-sighted—focusing on you and your plan for today. Thank you that I can know your plan for my life by doing your will day by day.

ARE YOU EARNEST ON PURPOSE?

And you will seek Me and find Me, when you search for Me with all your heart.
Jeremiah 29:13, *NASB*

If you were to die today, would you have accomplished the purpose for which you were born?

What would you say is the purpose of your life? How would you define your ultimate purpose and your unique personal purpose?

How do you think God would answer those questions about each of us? He has a primary purpose for all of us which we share in common. But He also has a secondary purpose for each individual to accomplish which is a part of that primary purpose.

I have found it a rigorous but, eventually, releasing discipline to refocus my purpose—repeatedly. When I am able to recapture the reason I was given life, I experience a new freedom to live with joy and abandon. In that context, I can honestly say that if I were to expire today, I have discovered the reason I was born. Then I can rediscover the personalized purpose of my life. This liberates me to prioritize the opportunities and challenges of daily living.

When either our ultimate or unique purpose becomes clouded or confused, we find that we lose an essential quality of life: earnestness. We are no longer direct, zealous, fervent. Earnestness is distinguished by deep feeling and conviction, resoluteness and dedication.

When we drift from a deep, intimate companionship with God, we become negative, critical, judgmental and recalcitrant. We resist the repeated overtures of God's love. Neutrality and detached aloofness eventually result. We become respectably unresponsive. It happens to all of us at times. The telltale signs are equivocation, vacillation and pretense.

That's what happened to the Pharisees. They rejected John the Baptist and resisted Jesus' ministry. Don't forget that they were the religious leaders of the time. What happened to them, can happen to us. We can get just enough religion to make us rigid, but lose our purpose which releases power.

I talked to a church officer in a midwest church recently who had drifted from earnestness to equivocation. He said, "I am sure about what I don't want, but I don't know what I want. I'm against about everything that's proposed, but I am at a loss when challenged to make a positive suggestion for what we should be doing. I fuss over insignificant details of church administration and

137

have become critical of almost everyone and everything." What a pitiful condition.

Be sure of this: if we don't know where we are going, we will be negative and critical of where others want to go. The issue is our relationship to Christ and our surrender to His guidance and direction. Church boards can be like a marketplace with opposing factions childishly complaining, "You weren't for my motion, so I won't be for yours." All because the Lord was disregarded and denied complete control. Exciting things happen to individuals and congregations when we are earnest about the Lord of the church.

A woman came to me about her marriage. She was sure her husband was her problem. She said, "If my husband would only change, we could make a go of this marriage."

I listened to her dissatisfied complaints for what seemed like hours. Finally I asked her to list 10 things she wanted her husband to do and be. In a subsequent visit with her husband I tried to communicate her needs to him. We talked at length about what it would take to satisfy her demands. He made a commitment to try. I kept close contact to see how things were going. The man made every effort to change, but whatever he did, it was not enough.

Weeks later, the wife came to see me again. She blurted out, "Now what am I going to do? My husband has met all my demands, but I'm still unhappy. What's wrong with me?"

The answer to that question was in her relationship with Christ. Though the woman was an active church member, she had never given Christ complete control of her life and relationships. All her religious activity was a smoke screen for her lack of commitment to Christ. Her husband's efforts to change only exposed her own need to change. Underneath her words was the deep desire to get

138

out of the marriage. She was too religious to think of divorce. When her husband became a Christian and began growing spiritually, her own lack of earnestness was exposed. I'm happy to say that's not the end of the story. At a Day of Discovery Retreat sponsored by our congregation, she met the Savior about whom she had talked and organized activities for so long. Now she knows what she wants and wants whom she knows.

I was deeply gratified by the statement of one of my members who visited me the other day. "Lloyd, something happened to me in church last week. I felt the presence of the Lord as I sat in the pew. When you said, 'The living Lord is here!' I said to myself, 'That's really true.' I had come to worship not really expecting to either meet Him or sense His special touch on my life. But as the service proceeded, I was made aware of all the areas of my life that had never been brought under the guidance and control of the Lord. That's why I'm here today. I want to take the Lord seriously."

That's it! To take the Lord seriously. What would that mean? Does the Lord have charge of all that there is of us? Our hearts, relationships, jobs, money, hopes and plans? He wants nothing less!

Recently my congregation decided to give a special offering to world missions. Each of us was challenged to ask the Lord to guide us in the amount—above our regular giving pledge—we would make. We had to dare to believe that the Lord would guide an amount that He would provide. Some very exciting things happened. Many people made pledges beyond what they anticipated their income would allow. An excitement swept throughout our congregation as people's earnestness was rewarded by monies from unexpected sources. The Lord guided the pledge and provided the means.

One woman wrote me, "I'm on a fixed income. I was astonished when I felt led to pledge an additional amount for missions because I had no idea where the money would come from. A week later, I got a check in the mail for the exact amount I had pledged. Isn't God good! All He needed was an open channel to pass the money through." The woman had been earnest and the earnest Lord of all creation unleashed the money because she could be trusted to do what she had promised.

The same is true of the unlimited power of the Holy Spirit. He waits for us to dare to attempt things beyond our strength and talents. When we do He provides wisdom, faith, discernment and resources we never dreamed were available. If we take Him seriously, our life will be punctuated by miracles.

A couple I know have a gift of healing. I have kept a documented list of the spectacular physical, emotional and spiritual healings God has done through these two. We lunch frequently to swap stories of God's interventions. Each time I am refreshed and renewed by the evidences of the relationship between their earnestness to trust the promises of God and the results in blessings to people. These adventurers really believe that God is faithful to His promises. They have drawn on the untapped resources of God because they fervently believe that the purpose of their lives is to care for people. They know what they need and need what they want.

The earnest Lord of all says, "For I know the plans that I have for you . . . plans for welfare and not for calamity to give you a future and a hope. Then you will call upon Me and come and pray to Me, and I will listen to you. And you will seek Me and find Me, when you search for Me with all your heart" (Jer. 29:11-13, *NASB*). There's a purpose which demands an earnestness now and for all eternity. Instead of playing games, we have a game plan for a truly exciting life.

Savior, I view your earnest and purposeful trek to the cross as a model for my daily, living response to my salvation. May I be as wholeheartedly devoted to my tasks as you are to yours.

DELIGHTING IN DUTY

I delight to do Thy will, O my God; Thy law is within my heart. Psalm 40:8, *NASB*

———————————◆———————————

I was called to the hospital late in the night. A highly respected member of my congregation was in serious condition. He was suffering from a terminal disease and was not expected to live. His outstanding career in the business world had distinguished him, and his contributions in the church and community had made him a very highly respected person. He had been a tireless worker in Christian causes, a tither of his sizable income, and an admired example of Christian character.

When I arrived on his floor of the hospital I found his room was next to an infamous criminal. There were policemen outside the door. Inquiry revealed that the prisoner had been shot in an exchange of gunfire at the time of his arrest for robbery. A patrolman had been killed in the line of duty by him. The prisoner had a bullet lodged in his chest. The prognosis was that he would live to stand trial. When I learned his name, I identified him as a person whose irresponsible life had been marked by a long line of petty thievery, rape and imprisonments.

My friend and the prisoner couldn't have been more different. One was a contributor to society; the other a leech. My parishioner had made his mark for upbuilding the community; the criminal had become a blight on everything good and creative. Why was one, who had paid his dues to society's improvement, dying, and one, who has wasted his life, going to live?

I sat in the waiting room with my member's wife. She was asking the same question. I waited with her through the excruciating vigil of anxiety. All that could be said to her had been communicated. I tried to give comfort and courage. The pain of uncertainty about her husband's prognosis and the nerve-jangling anxiety stretched into the dawn hours of a new day. Exhaustion and frustration finally released her to say what she was thinking and I was feeling. I noted her wringing her hands. Her eyes dilated to pinpoint precision. She swung around in her chair and met me eyeball to eyeball. Her voice was staccato and piercing.

"Listen, Pastor. You'd better talk to God. There are two people on this floor in serious condition. One is going to live and the other die. It's not fair! That criminal has no right to live and my husband has. You should tell God that my husband has a break coming. He's spent his life working for God. He has given himself doing good for years. He deserves a break. God owes him a big, fat miracle; and I expect you to tell Him so. If that criminal lives and my husband dies, it will prove there's no justice or reward in this life!"

My response was to tell her about God's love and to comfort her in her grief. I reminded her that her husband had not done good to build up a reserve of preferential treatment. The Lord was not finished with either of the critical patients on that floor. He would deal with both in His own way. Death would not be an ending for her beloved. Comparisons were irrelevant. Each of us passes through the narrow door of God's judgment individually. But God would not pull off an impossibility for one because he was good and condemn another because he was bad. He wanted both to live forever.

The long drive home from the hospital, as the sun began to rise, gave me time to reflect on what the woman had said. She spoke out of duress, but beneath her expression of the seeming injustice of it all, was a firmly held presupposition. She believed life was a balance scale. Her husband had done his part loading his side of the scale. Now it was God's turn. Or was it? Her words tumbled about in my mind. They sparked other memories of familiar statements about the system of rewards by which so many people live.

I heard the often-repeated sentiments: "What did I do to deserve this? After all I've done for God and people, why did this happen to me?" The same confused convictions pervade our relationships: "I give and give, and nobody seems to appreciate my efforts." "I give my wife all she wants and she never considers what I need!" "Nobody seems to recognize my efforts—my kids, my fellow workers, my friends at church." "What's the use? Who cares that I do what's right and give myself and my resources to make this a better world?" Sound familiar? Ever feel that way? Who hasn't?

We expect rewards. It's built into our system of give and take. Life has its duties, relationships, their obligations, and work its responsibilities. But what should we expect in return? Most of us love to be loved, give to receive, work to be praised and paid handsomely.

It's a part of our ethic. Whole schools of psychology have been built around the idea that personality is shaped by strokes and patterned by pats on the back. B.F. Skinner has shown us the power of reinforcement, or lack of it, for behavior modification. Eric Berne has exposed the games people play and revealed the power of strengthening strokes. We all know about the enabling initiative of affirmation to encourage people in a pattern of behavior which is in keeping with what we want from them. Our childhood training has engrained the I'll-love-you-if syndrome in our psyches.

We project that to God. Our belief is that we can store up a spiritual savings account to draw on when life levels its blows. We think our goodness conditions His grace on our crises. The distressed wife in the waiting room articulated our prejudice more than we may want to admit!

Jesus believed in and practiced the power of affirmation. He gave people a liberating image of who they were because of God's love. But He did not teach a system of bartered goodness and rewards.

That's hard for us to accept. The whole fiber of our life is woven by the back-and-forth movement of the shuttle of our works and expected rewards from God. We think that He will love us if we are good, bless us if we are effective, care for us if we are efficient. We barter for His acceptance. We promise to stop some habit if He will give us what we want. We will do a loving and forgiving thing to be sure we can count on His approval. Our prayers are a negotiation for the best deal we can get. Giving money is to be assured of financial success. Acts of mercy are to insure that we will be given His mercy. But God owes us

145

nothing—whatever we do for Him. After all we've done we still must say, "We are unworthy servants. We did only what was our duty."

The piercing point in this: The thing we do for rewards, we should do because it's our duty. That's not a popular word in our time. We hear a lot about freedom and grace these days. What we do does not earn salvation, we are told. True. But the result is that many of us do very little. We presume. Christians gather in churches every Sunday to collect "unemployment compensation." The sanctuary is a "duty free" shop for bargains.

So much that is needed in our society is a part of basic Christianity. We should not need special motivation for honesty, integrity, righteousness and justice. That ought to be as normal as breathing, eating and sleeping. Expressing love and forgiveness should not be a big thing. It's basic Christianity. Feeding the hungry and caring for the poor doesn't warrant a brass band recognition. Allowing the plumb line of Christ's message to fall on our decisions and policies in business is normal Christian living. Why are we so excited when some Christ-oriented, biblically-guided Christian does a costly act of obedience? Big deal! After we've done what's required, we still must say: We are unworthy servants; we did only what was our duty.

Beyond duty is delight. And delight transforms how we do our duties. Faith is its own reward. There is a joy we experience when we serve the Master before ourselves. To put Christ first in our lives enables a breakthrough from a duty-bound life.

Paul caught the exuberance of this: "For in my inner being I delight in God's law" (Rom. 7:22, *NIV*). He went on to say that His delight was constantly at war with the lesser motivation of obligation. We all know what that's

146

like. We need a fresh release each day to live our lives motivated by love alone, not by calculated self-justification. Delighting in God Himself and what He's done for us transforms how we do our duties. It does not exonerate us from responsibility; it enthuses us to live and act as a response to amazing grace.

Then we can pray like the old Scott: "Lord, this is John, reporting in for duty." And there will be fresh assignments every day. We'll never be finished. The sense of unworthiness will come not from disobedience, but from the realization that we have only touched the surface of what needs to be done. But what is done will be accomplished with delight!

Striding into life with you is not a job, Lord, it's a joy! Thank you for the delight of partnership with you in ministry.

PRAYING INTO GOD'S HAND

It shall come to pass that before they call, I will answer; And while they are still speaking, I will hear. Isaiah 65:24, *NKJV*

I want to share a revolutionary thought. It has changed my life. My whole perception of prayer has been transformed by it. As a result, my prayers and praying have become more exciting than ever.

I've been a Christian for over forty years. Far too many of those years were spent with a totally incorrect conception of prayer. I labored with the misapprehension that prayer was my idea, that conversation with God was initiated by me. That idea took on the heavy baggage of believing that I had to get God's attention and that He would listen and respond if I said the right words and led a life worthy of His condescension. Prayer became burdensome, laborious. Often I was reluctant to pray when I needed to the most because of things I'd done or said which made me feel ashamed or embarrassed by a less than perfect life. The conception that prayer was initiated by me left it up to my moods and spiritual readiness.

Then one day a few years ago, I happened on a combination of Scriptures from the Old and New Testaments which exploded the tight, constricted, and limited view of prayer I had held. They all thundered forth a truth which I desperately needed to learn and live.

Stated simply it is this: prayer starts with God. It is His idea. The desire to pray is the result of God's greater desire to talk with us. He has something to say when we feel the urge to pray. He is the initiator. The keen desire to begin and end the day with prolonged prayer is His gift. The sense of need to pray for challenges or opportunities throughout the day is because He has wisdom and insight He wants to impart. When we face crises and suddenly feel the urge to pray for strength, that feeling is a response to the Lord's invasion of our minds which triggers the thought of needing help which is congealed into the desire to pray. He, not us, was the author of the longing for His help.

Listen to what the Lord Himself tells us about prayer. "It shall come to pass that before they call, I will answer; And while they are still speaking, I will hear" (Isa. 65:24, *NKJV*). That tells us that the answer to our prayers is prepared before we pray. The desire to talk to the Lord about our needs comes from Him. Prayer begins in the mind of God, invades our minds, is formulated into a clarification of what He wants to do or give, and then is articulated in our words. He is more ready to hear than we are to pray!

Thomas Carlyle once said, "Prayer is and remains a

149

native and deep impulse of the soul of man." That sounds lovely, but I don't believe it. No one naturally desires to pray. Our volitional capacity is debilitated until we are loved, liberated, and regenerated by Christ. It is after we have been transformed by the cross and filled with the Spirit that we can experience the enlivening of the "native and deep impulse" to pray. And even after we've been born again, it is the Lord who motivates us to pray. It is part of His prevenient, beforehand grace. Not even the longing for God is our accomplishment. It is birthed in our souls by the Lord who created us for communion with Him.

Commenting on this promise in Isaiah, Luther said, "Our prayer pleases God because He has commanded it, made promises, and given form to our prayer. For that reason, He is pleased with our prayer. He requires it and delights in it, because He promises, commands, and shapes it . . . Then He says, 'I will hear.' It is not only guaranteed, but it is actually already obtained."[2]

Recently I had a misunderstanding with a cherished friend which resulted in a broken relationship. The startling thing was that for a time I didn't want to find a reconciliation. I chalked it up to irreconcilable differences which precluded the possibility of forgiveness and a new beginning. I was hurt and angry. My plan was to forget the whole mess. Some weeks later, an uneasiness began to grow in me. I couldn't shake the man out of my mind. That was followed by a mysterious desire to pray about him. When I responded to the inner urgings to pray, I noticed a difference in my attitude.

As I prayed, I was given new empathy for what might have caused the man's behavior. I was given a completely different picture of the needs inside him; and then I asked for a way to communicate acceptance and forgiveness. As

150

I lingered in prayer, a strategy was unfolded for what I needed to do and say. I had the deep conviction that the plan came from the Lord. Therefore when I asked for His help to accomplish His will in the matter, I could ask with boldness. The inner disquiet, like an inaudible wordless groaning, turned into clarity and was articulated in a request for strength to do what the Lord had promised He would do through me if I were willing. A new, ready will worked with my imagination to form the picture of how it would be accomplished. And that's exactly the way it turned out. The Lord was initiator and inspiration from start to finish.

Prayer starts with God. Our desire to pray is the result of His call to prayer. He has something to say. Our responsibility is to listen to what He wants to give us for our problems and potentials. He will make it clear. Then we can say with boldness:

> I sought the Lord, and afterward I knew
>   He moved my soul to seek Him, seeking me;
> It was not I that found, O Savior true,
>   No, I was found of Thee.[3]

You want to commune with me, Lord, and I am moved at the thought. Help me respond with an ever-widening openness and ever-deepening commitment to vital communication.

GOD'S TRANSFORMING LOVE

He Helps Me Through Trials

Trouble for me tests the extent to which I am living a supernatural life. I believe the world should be astounded by what the Lord does with us in trouble. In it we discover that the Lord is able.

TRIUMPHING OVER TROUBLE

The salvation of the righteous comes from the Lord; he is their stronghold in time of trouble. Psalm 37:39, *NIV*

The musical Annie is a couple of hours of sheer delight and an affirmation of life. Little Orphan Annie infuses hope and positive expectation in everyone from Daddy Warbucks to F.D.R. with enthusiastic singing of the theme song, "Tomorrow." The words have lingered in my mind ever since I had the relaxing pleasure of hearing of Annie's simple trust that things will be different in our tomorrows.

The sun'll come out tomorrow
Bet your bottom dollar
That tomorrow there'll be sun,

155

Just thinkin' about tomorrow
Clears away the cobwebs and the sorrow
Till there's none.[1]

As I was leaving the theater with these words tumbling about in my mind, I overheard a man say to his wife, "I sure feel better after that! Funny thing, I forgot my troubles for two solid hours. Maybe the sun will come out tomorrow for us."

Strange, isn't it, how a simple song of hope can lift people out of discouragement with life's troubles. Trouble is a universal experience. Everybody has some. No one is exempt. It comes to young and old, rich and poor, talented and inept, believers and nonbelievers, people inside and outside the church.

Will the sun really come out tomorrow? Will tomorrow be better than today? Will we get a breakthrough to new hope for our troubles? What happens when yesterday's troubles blend into today's troubles and we are left with little expectation for a different tomorrow? We say, "Annie's song was great for Broadway and Hollywood theater, but isn't that nothing more than a simplistic wish-dream?" How can we endure in our troubles when the clouds don't break open for the sun to shine through?

Mark Twain was right. "Trouble has done it. Bilgewater, trouble has done it; trouble has brung these gray hairs and this premature balditude." But it does more than that: it wears us down, takes the zest out of life and brings us to that discouraged state wherein we begin to expect trouble as the inevitable stuff of life. Some people get so used to trouble that they are uneasy without it and inadvertently do things to perpetuate its uncomfortable tension. George Herbert said, "He that seeks trouble never misses."

My definition of trouble is anything which disrupts our

156

dreams. Big troubles are those which interrupt our life plan and purposes; little troubles are distressing fouls setting back any day's game plan. We can grapple with the latter but it's the former which wear us down. It is the diversion of the flow of life from our goals into an eddy of disappointment that gets to us.

Few of us could say that life has turned out as we planned. Even those of us who would attest that life has developed infinitely better than we could ever have imagined would have to admit that it has not been without troubles. We've all experienced the hard discipline of desires denied and visions vanquished. But we are in good company. The spiritual giants of Scripture and the adventuresome saints of history became the frontiersmen they were because of how they handled trouble. They all knew the agitating addition of trouble to their life agendas.

We are forced to grapple with the causes of trouble. We bring a lot of it on ourselves. Poor judgment, unguided decisions, selfishness, pride and negativism all contribute to our self-made troubles. People are the second major cause of trouble. Who doesn't have his or her share of troublesome people who either stand in the way of our moving forward to our dreams and plans or who agitate the flow of our river of life with whirlpools of their personal confusion?

Another cause of trouble comes in life's sicknesses, reversals, broken relationships, loss of loved ones, and fractured hopes. The closed doors of circumstances trouble all of us. But there's a deeper reason we have troubles. We are God's beloved people who must live in a fallen creation in which Satan is a persistent troublemaker for those who belong to the Lord. He can take all the other sources of trouble and use them to unsettle our confidence both in the Lord and ourselves.

Faith grows in trouble. I know that from my own life. It has made me depend on the Lord. He constantly presses me out into new challenges in which I have no visible means of support. But I have Him! In trouble I've learned to depend on the promise of two of my life verses. "Let not your heart be troubled" (John 14:1, *NKJV*); "I am leaving you with a gift—peace of mind and heart! And the peace I give isn't fragile like the peace the world gives. So don't be troubled or afraid. Remember what I told you . . . I will come . . . to you" (John 14:27,28, *TLB*).

Trouble for me tests the extent to which I am living a supernatural life. I believe the world should be astounded by what the Lord does with us in trouble. In it we discover that the Lord is able. The trumpet blast of the New Testament Church is that He is able. He is with us when we are tempted to give up. "He is able to aid those who are tempted" (Heb. 2:18, *NKJV*).

Christ is our High Priest making intercession for our strength in trouble. "He is also able to save to the uttermost those who come to God through Him, since He ever lives to make intercession for them" (Heb. 7:25, *NKJV*). He will never allow trouble to defeat us. "Now to Him who is able to keep you from stumbling, and to present you faultless before the presence of His glory with exceeding joy" (Jude 24, *NKJV*).

His power is greater than Satan's beguiling use of discouragement. "He is able even to subdue all things to Himself" (Phil. 3:21, *NKJV*). He keeps His promise to overcome the demons of despair when we surrender our troubles to Him and are willing to grow through them. "For I know whom I have believed and am persuaded that He is able to keep what I have committed to Him until that Day" (2 Tim. 1:12, *NKJV*).

Trouble gives us an opportunity to discover the triumphant sufficiency of His power at work in us. "Now to Him who is able to do exceedingly abundantly above all that we ask or think, according to the power that works in us" (Eph. 3:20, *NKJV*). Our hope in trouble is not that we are able, but that He is able. The Son will come out, and in, today!

What confidence to know, Victorious Lord, that a seed of triumph is germinating within each trouble I face. I anticipate your activity in me as we tackle trouble together.

CALL ME COURAGEOUS

Be strong and take heart, all you who hope in the Lord. Psalm 31:24, NIV

If we are not attempting something which creates the human reaction of fear we are probably not living life as it was meant to be lived. Fear in the soul-stretching challenges drives us to prayer. Eddie Rickenbacker, famous American pilot, knew what he was talking about when he said that courage is doing what you're afraid to do. There is no courage unless you're scared and are driven to your knees.

Thomas Fuller, English divine and author (1608-1661), said, "Fear can keep a man out of danger, but courage can support him in it." The psalmist discovered the Lord's antidote to fear when he heard Him say in the depth of his soul, "Call upon me in the day of trouble: I will deliver thee, and thou shalt glorify me" (Ps. 50:15, *KJV*). Like all of us, he wanted to escape life's challenges. "Oh that I had wings like a dove! for then would I fly away, and be at rest" (Ps. 55:6, *KJV*). But honest praying had not allowed such a flight from reality and responsibility.

Prayer is not an escape but an encounter. Nehemiah discovered that when his frightened friends encouraged him to check out from the endless conflict and discouragement of rebuilding the walls of Jerusalem. His response should be a memorized motto for us: "Should a man like me flee? And could one such as I go into the temple to save his life?" (Neh. 6:11, *NASB*).

Thomas Carlyle, Scottish historian, said that life begins with the quiet estimate of ourselves that will not let us play the coward. And that quiet estimate of our fear and the Lord's power is the essence of authentic prayer.

Remember the timing of the Lord when the people of Israel had to cross the Jordan and go into the Promised Land? He told Joshua that when the priests carrying the ark put their feet in the water, He would roll back the Jordan so they could pass through. Experience that from within the skin of one of those priests! The first step into the water must have been difficult. But when the soles of their feet were wet, the Lord opened the way through the riverbed. Joshua and those priests anguished over the pain of answered prayer. And so do we. It is when the soles of our feet are wet with the first step of obedience that courage is given and the way opens for us.

Authentic courage is something we take because the Lord has taken hold of us. Courage is an offered gift which we must take. The psalmist discovered that. The Lord said to him, "Be strong, and let your heart take courage"

(Ps. 31:24, *NASB*). Courage is ours for the taking. It must be claimed and appropriated. This is the salient thrust of Jesus' offer to His disciples on the night before the Crucifixion.

I like the accurate rendering of the Greek in the *New American Standard Bible*. "These things I have spoken to you, that in Me you may have peace. In the world you have tribulation, but take courage; I have overcome the world" (John 16:33). This translation is stronger than others which say, "Be of good cheer." The word is *tharseite* in Greek, active imperative. It comes from *tharsos*, courage. The imperative carries the challenge to "take courage." We can take it only because the Lord has taken us. He has a tight grip on us.

Think of the crucial times this offer is made in the New Testament. It was spoken to the paralytic in Matthew 9:2 (*NASB*) when the Lord said, "Take courage . . . your sins are forgiven." The same assurance was spoken to the woman who pressed through the crowd and touched the Master. "Take courage, your faith has made you well" (Matt. 9:22, *NASB*). The people around blind Bartimaeus said it when Jesus responded to his plea. "Take courage . . . He is calling for you" (Mark 10:49, *NASB*).

In prayer, the Lord takes hold of us with one hand and offers courage with the other.

> Thy love to me, O God,
> Not mine, O Lord to Thee,
> Can rid me of this dark unrest
> And set my spirit free.
> Let me no more my comfort draw
> From my frail hold on Thee.
> Rather in this rejoice with awe
> Thy mighty grasp on me. [2]

DON'T GIVE UP— PRAY THROUGH!

I pray that out of his glorious riches he may strengthen you with power through his Spirit in your inner being.
Ephesians 3:16, *NIV*

There are two very different ways of saying, "I'm finished!" One is the triumphant expression of the delight of completion. The other is the discouraged admission of defeat. So often it is the latter. Life is littered with unfinished tasks, uncompleted goals, unfulfilled assignments, and unhealed relationships.

Living is like a race with many laps. Each lap is made up of tasks given us to do. In His providential management of life, the Lord gives each of us challenges which only we can do. And in our efforts to accomplish His assignment, we are often tempted to give up before we are finished.

We've all known times when we were tempted to give up on people, prospects, and demanding opportunities. Perhaps we are breathlessly running one of those laps right now. We are not sure we are going to make it. We need a second wind, or what joggers call the "runner's high" when suddenly new strength is given and we are able to exceed our natural capacities.

It is in prayer that we put our roots down deeply into the limitless reservoir of God's strength. When we tell the Lord we are tempted to give up, that we are dangerously close to being engulfed with our problems, then He gives us the stamina to keep on steadfastly.

A clergy friend of mine was tempted to quit. He was drained and depleted. In despair, he went to a spiritually sensitive older friend. She empathized, and then put her finger on the raw nerve. "You are like a pump unconnected to a well. People have pumped you dry. Your greatest need is to reestablish contact with the Lord. People need Him, not your knowledge, adequacy or cleverness. Instead of quitting, take a week off for silence with the Lord. Allow Him to heal your hurts and meet your needs. Stop working for the Lord and let Him work through you."

The man was stunned by the woman's directness. The Lord was at work and gave him the honesty to accept the piercing advice. He secured a retired pastor to fill his pulpit the following Sunday and went into the mountains for a full-week retreat of silence. Exhausted in body and soul, he slept for the first full day and night. Then he began to allow the Lord to refocus his life's purpose and goals. That was followed with long walks in which he asked the Lord to show him what He wanted him to do to complete the lap of his life in the parish he was serving. Most of all, he allowed the Lord to meet his own needs for replenishment.

The clergyman returned to work a new man. With his priorities redefined, he reestablished his own time of daily prayer and meditation which had previously been edged out by busy-ness. The greatest gift he could give his congregation was to do more than say his prayers; to spend prolonged time in prayer. He began living in the stream of the Lord's power.

The result was that he now had an indefatigable supply of inspiration and wisdom as well as joy and hope to give to his people. He is finishing the lap of renewing his present parish. After that the Lord will have another lap for him to run. He told me that his fondest hope is that he will never forget what he's discovered in this lap of the race.

Winston Churchill said in dark days when his countrymen were tempted to become discouraged, "Never give in! Never give in! Never, never, never—in anything great or small, large or petty—never give in except to convictions of honor and good sense." To take and apply that admonition we need more than human pertinacity; we need God-given perseverance.

James reminds us that faith without works is dead. So too, prayer without work is ineffective. But equally so, work without consistent prayer will wear us out. The Lord never assigns us more to do than we can accomplish with His replenishing power. He guides the task, gives the strength to do it, and keeps us going until we finish. Don't give up!

Lord, deliver me from the dangerous misconception that I must struggle through life alone. I welcome today a fresh insight into the exercise of tenacious prayer by which I tap into your power.

THE POWER OF EVERYWHERE PRAYER

I want men everywhere to lift up holy hands
in prayer, without anger or disputing.
1 Timothy 2:8, *NIV*

———————————❖———————————

B ased on his own experiences of the omnipresence and omniscience of his ubiquitous, ever-present Lord, Paul challenged people to pray everywhere. That covers the whole range of life's experiences. Alone, with people, at home, on the job, making money or making love, on vacation or in the battles of life.

Psalm 139 describes David's experience of the "every-whereness" of the Lord. "Where can I go from Your Spirit? Or where can I flee from Your presence? If I ascend into heaven, You are there; If I make my bed in hell, behold, You are there. If I take the wings of the morning, and dwell in the uttermost parts of the sea, Even there

Your hand shall lead me, And Your right hand shall hold me. If I say, 'Surely the darkness shall fall on me,' Even the night shall be light about me; Indeed, the darkness shall not hide from You, but the night shines as the day; The darkness and the light are both alike to You" (Ps. 139:7-12, *NKJV*). The Lord of all life is not only always available for prayer, but He is inescapable. And in each moment He is calling us into prayer so that His best can be given to us and the people around us.

I find it helpful to think of prayer everywhere like breathing. All through the day I try to remember to breathe out the prayer, "Lord, I need you!" and then breathe in with the prayer of receptive gratitude, "Lord, I receive you!" It works wonders while studying or writing, talking with people, in staff or official board meetings, as well as in trying times of difficulty. Our minds are amazingly capable of doing several things at the same time. In a conversation, for example, we do not deny another person our full attention when at the same time we are praying for him or her. The same is true for preaching. While I am speaking I try to remember to pray all through the message that what is said will reach people's minds and hearts. When people listen and pray for what God wants to tell them through the message, powerful things happen. And the glory goes to the Lord!

A further aspect of Paul's word to Timothy that we should pray everywhere is that we should lift "holy hands . . . without anger or disputing." The Hebrew practice of lifting hands when in prayer, mentioned in the Old Testament (Neh. 8:6), is probably what Paul referred to. The practice is customary in some churches today. I've found it to be a helpful and tangibly physical way of claiming the Lord's presence and power in various situations in which I pray for help.

Once I was on a long flight from coast to coast. The hours had to be spent in a very strategic study and writing assignment. The need for clarity and accuracy was demanding. Often through the hours I would put my pen down, lift my arms and pray silently, "Lord, help me!" Later during the mealtime a woman across the aisle leaned over and said, "Sir, are you all right? You seem to be stretching a lot."

I laughed as I told her, "Yes, I was stretching, but also praying." She seemed interested in this gesture of prayer so I explained that what I was writing needed the Lord's word-for-word guidance and inspiration. That led to a visit about prayer and the Lord's intervening power in our affairs.

Just as the plane landed, she looked me in the eye and said, "I need you to do some stretching for me. I've got some difficult decisions to make in the next few days. Pray for me. And after what I've learned about prayer in our talk, you can be sure I'll be praying for the Lord's help. People in my office will probably think I'm stretching a lot also!" We both laughed and she went off to meet her particular set of impossibilities in which I am confident she discovered that with the Lord's intervention, all things are possible.

A friend of mine is a famous surgeon. He's also a committed Christian who believes that his skill is a gift of the Lord. The spiritual gift of healing is coupled with immense capabilities as a surgeon.

One day in the operating room, a relatively new assistant asked him a question. "Why is it that at the most strategic, life-and-death moment of the surgery you pause, put down your instruments and stretch?" He explained that in tedious operations like that he needed the Great Physician's help and he paused to pray that he would know the exact thing to do. This brilliant surgeon had learned that the Lord was with him and his powers were dependent on His guidance.

I have another friend who leans back in his chair and lifts his hands at crisis points in meetings in the board room of his company. He is praying for wisdom. His associates are aware that his most ingenious suggestions are made after one of those "stretching times."

We needn't press that gesture of supplication too far. The Lord is no more available if we lift our hands in claiming His help. What is important is developing a technique of praying in all circumstances, everywhere.

Thank you, Lord, for the encouragement that I am a living prayer chapel everywhere I go and that the extended hands of prayer always reach the storehouse of your provision.

JESUS, THE NAME THAT CHARMS OUR FEARS

There is no fear in love; but perfect love casts out fear. 1 John 4:18, *NKJV*

We all have fears which rob us of the joy of living. We fear certain people, failure, pain, and inadequacy. Beneath all our fears is the fear of losing control and the ability to cope. At the root of this fear is the fear of dying.

Charles Wesley (1707-1788) wrote beautifully about the power of the name to overcome our fears. "Jesus! the name that charms our fears, that bids our sorrows cease, 'tis music in the sinner's ears, 'tis life and health and peace."

170

How does Jesus Christ charm our fears? From my own personal experience He does it in several ways. First, He exposes them for what they are. He helps us ask, "Of what or whom am I afraid?" Then the Lord forces us to face the fear with a further question, "Does this person or situation have any power greater than Christ?" And then He lovingly asks, "Will you give me that fear and allow me to give you courage to overcome it?"

Fear is the outward manifestation of the feeling of insufficiency. We are afraid when we are unsure that we will have what it takes to live, face troubles, endure sickness, and die with assurance of eternal life. We worry over money because of previous shortages. We are troubled by certain kinds of people because of prior hurts by similar personality types. Failures in the past make us catatonic because we fear further failure.

Most of all fear is entangled with what has happened to us in the past. We need a healing of the memories in order to face the future unafraid. The secret of how the Lord does that is given us by the Apostle John. "There is no fear in love; but perfect love casts out fear, because fear involves torment. But he who fears has not been made perfect in love. We love Him because He first loved us" (1 John 4:18-19, *NKJV*).

Remember that the one who wrote these words had faced persecution, imprisonment, and constant danger. The remedial remedy for fear he gives us is one he had experienced through long years of communion with the living Lord. He had been the beloved disciple of the Lord, had depended on His love in excruciating circumstances, and had found Him triumphantly adequate in his trials. Most of all, he had seen and heard Him say, "Do not be afraid; I am the First and the Last. I am He who lives, and was dead, and behold, I am alive forevermore. Amen. And

171

I have the keys of Hades and of Death" (Rev. 1:17-18, *NKJV*).

Note the strong I am, spoken with the authority of Yahweh. He is the beginning and end of all things. He has conquered death and overcome the forces of evil. John found that consistent oneness with the Lord cast out his fears. His love in each potential fear displaced the fear.

Fear can best be defined as the absence of love. The same emotional channel through which fear is felt and expressed is also the channel of experiencing and communicating love. The conquest of our fears happens through a love relationship with our Lord. The more we allow Him to love us, the more free we will be of fear. Fear is feeling unloved or being anxious about the consistency and faithfulness of people's love. Christ's love for us is unchanging, unlimited, and unqualified. He, divine love, fills us with His Spirit and fear is displaced. Anytime we feel afraid, it is a sure sign we need to surrender the memory, circumstance, person, or danger to the Lord.

But the ultimate conquest of fear happens when we accept that nothing or no one can ultimately hurt us. We are alive forever. Our destiny is sure. And anything in between now and heaven will be used by the Lord to help us trust Him more fully. We are indestructible! The Lord has taken up residence in us and our true inner person will reign with Him now and through all of eternity. That's the source of true courage for all of life's battles.

The name of Jesus is more than a title or descriptive designation of His nature. The name is really sacramental in that it is an outward sign of a limitless power, authority, and presence. The word "sacrament" comes from the Latin *sacramentum,* a mystery. But it also was used for an oath or pledge of allegiance and obedience to Caesar by a Roman legionnaire. Ranking officers of the Roman armies carried a medallion of Caesar's authority. The idea conveyed was that wherever that officer went he could depend on all the authority and power of Rome to be marshalled in any conflict or battle. He had made his oath of obedience to Caesar and knew that the empire's power was available to be called forth.

In a much more propitious way the name of Jesus Christ, the Lord, gives us greater assurance. Through His name, mysteriously the power of God is released for our needs, complexities, and fears. We are not alone. Our sacred symbol is the cross. The same victorious power revealed there and vindicated in the resurrection is ours. The faithful prayer in the name of the Lord brings the effluence of His Spirit, His wisdom for our decisions, His strength for our weaknesses, and His love for our fears. And in addition to that, He goes before us to invade our difficulties. He deals with people long before we meet them, and unravels problems long before we confront them. Our Lord is able!

———————⋄—⋇—⋄———————

Fill me so completely with your love today, Lord Jesus, that my fears—great and small—are squeezed out and washed away.

HANGING IN WHEN YOU'D RATHER CHECK OUT

Be strong and very courageous.
Joshua 1:7, *NIV*

It was one of those "what's-the-use-why-stay-in-the-battle" kind of days. I was one of the speakers at a conference on church renewal at a small hotel in the mountains. The church leaders from various denominations seemed to be committed to church business as usual. Resistance to change permeated the atmosphere. The gray grimness of defensive institutional religion was written on people's joyless faces. Any efforts to infuse enthusiasm and capture an exciting vision were accepted with pleasant resistance. The woe of the status quo was shouted from the body language of the group.

174

"Why am I here?" I asked myself. I longed for the charade to end so I could go home to my "let's-go-pull-out-all-the-stops" congregation.

Halfway through the conference I left the meetings to take a walk. As I passed through the lobby of the hotel, I was startled to hear my name spoken by the telephone operator at the switchboard behind the registration counter.

"I'm sorry," she said, "Dr. Ogilvie has checked out."

I went over to her to tell her that, indeed, I had not checked out and that I had two more days reserved with the hotel.

"There must be some mistake, sir," the befuddled woman said. "According to our records, you've already checked out."

There was a mix-up with both registration and housekeeping. The error was corrected and I went on my walk.

As I strolled along a mountain path, it suddenly hit me. The telephone operator's statement was more prophetic than she had realized. I had checked out! Not from the hotel, but from the conference. I knew that a breakthrough to real communication would require the pain of encounter and possible conflict. Exposing false gods of religious people is a strenuous responsibility. Did I want to go through it again? How much did I really care about these frightened churchmen?

Then it dawned on me, I had the same need they had. We all needed courage. I needed a fresh infusion to confront the core of the need in my new friends at the conference and they needed it to go back to their churches to lead a profound renaissance. In a way we all had checked out!

Are you ever tempted to check out from life's battles and tensions? We all have times when we wonder if it's worth the strain. Often we check out from discipleship when the cost of caring becomes exorbitantly high. Or we check out on difficult people or demanding situations. We are still with them but have checked out mentally, emotionally or spiritually. The temptation to give up while we are still in the battle is constantly before us.

The thing I realized on my walk that afternoon is that we all live on the edge of equivocation and need courage. When I got in touch with my feelings, I realized that there was a next step in my pilgrimage that I needed and had been reluctant to take. The sure sign that we are in an authentic relationship with Christ is that there is a bold stride we need to take in being faithful and obedient. He is constantly pressing us on to new adventure where only His courage can sustain us. The more honest I became about where I needed courage, the more sensitive and empathetic I became during the rest of that conference. The Lord helped me open up with the people about my own fears and need for courage. I checked back in. You guessed it—there was a vital breakthrough and by the end of the time together the Lord blessed us all with a fresh touch of His power.

Your word, Dear Lord, coaxes my halting, hesitant steps into bold, courageous strides of obedient activity in your kingdom. I want to stay on the growing edge of what you are doing today.

TAP INTO GOD'S SUPPLY OF ENDURANCE

Endure hardship with us like a good soldier of Christ Jesus. 2 Timothy 2:3, NIV

The very week in which I am writing this has been a personal time of growth in endurance. I began the week with worries about the finances for my church's television ministry. Launching this outreach mission has forced me to trust the Lord completely. Monday was a troublesome day of surrendering the project again. On Tuesday I had lunch with a faithful giver to the program. He told me that he had had the television ministry on his heart.

He had prayed. "Lord, if this venture is your will for us, give me a sign." He was led to put out a fleece by placing a condominium he owned on the market, with the promise to the Lord that he would give the profit to the television fund. The substantial amount the Lord put in his mind was exactly what was needed to proceed with further production. The gift would be dependent on the sale of the property at the price the man was led to establish for the property. If he were to sell it for less, the profit would be less than what we needed. Because of the tight money market and the high interest rates for mortgages, a quick sale seemed unlikely.

We paused over lunch to pray. The Lord knew our need not only for the full amount but for a renewed sign of His affirmation of the ministry. We surrendered the whole trouble to Him.

The very next day a buyer purchased the property for cash! We should not have been surprised. The Lord knew the urgency. Three wonderful things resulted from the miracle. First, the Lord used the intervention to assure me that the television ministry was indeed His will for me and the church. The fleece was wringing wet! Second, the exact amount needed taught us again that the Lord knows our need and delights to astound us with His timeliness. Third, endurance was imbued. If He loved us that much in this need, we could trust Him with all our troubles! Now at the end of the week, I'm engrossed in new challenges and am tackling them with the fresh gusto of this week's miracle.

God gives us those special assurances to strengthen the muscle of our endurance. Outward trouble is to the Christian what tempests are to the oak tree. They serve to make the roots stronger. Trouble can temporarily rob us of tranquility or a smooth, easy life, but the only thing they can't take from us is our right to choose what our attitude will be. I am convinced that the true need of our hearts is the heart of our needs. And Christ satisfies that need with the gift of endurance. In trouble we move from the world's idea of peace to the peace of Christ.

"Therefore, having been justified by faith, we have peace with God through our Lord Jesus Christ, through whom also we have access by faith into this grace in which we stand, and rejoice in hope of the glory of God. And not only that, but we also glory in tribulations, knowing that tribulation produces perseverance; and perseverance, character; and character, hope. Now hope does not disappoint, because the love of God has been poured out in our hearts by the Holy Spirit who was given to us" (Rom. 5:1-5, *NKJV*).

Any trouble is worth it if in our struggle we are brought into that quality of peace. Troubles break the syndrome of independence and willfulness and bring us back to our Lord. At that moment of trust, endurance that lasts is given. Look, the Son has come out!

Often my endurance seems to wane in the swirling pressures which storm my spirit. Thank you, Strong Deliverer, for the accessible gift of endurance which buoys me above my circumstances.

HEALING FROM GOD'S HAND

Surely he took up our infirmities and carried our sorrows. Isaiah 53:4, *NIV*

———————————◆———————————

A man shared with me a very moving experience he had in the sanctuary during the worship one Sunday evening.

He said, "I had come to the service with a great need for healing in my spiritual and physical life. During the opening prayer I told the Lord how much I needed Him. I felt completely devoid of power. Then as you were finishing up the sermon, I felt a hand on my shoulder. I looked around to see if someone in the pew behind me was touching me or was trying to get my attention. The people behind me smiled but clearly indicated that they had not touched my shoulder. Then it happened again. After that I felt a warmth surge through my body. I felt the hand that had touched my shoulder was now connected to an arm that was joined by another arm to embrace me. I felt loved, accepted, cared about deeply. The Lord was answering the prayer I had prayed about my needs. I felt His Spirit surging through me. The tensions in my mind relaxed, my body felt calm, and my emotions were filled with joy. It was as if an electric current passed through every fibre of my being. Could it be that I received a touch from the Lord?"

It is important to mention that this man is a brilliant intellectual who is not highly emotional or spiritually expressive. He is a down-to-earth, practical, straightforward kind of man. In fact, he is reserved, sometimes very cautious, and genuinely scientific about the way he talks about evidence in any realm. When he went to his doctor the following week, the physical illness from which he had been suffering had radically improved. Subsequently, in the weeks that followed, he was completely healed. This was not in contradiction to the medical aid he was receiving, but a divine intervention which maximized what the medical profession was trying to do to help him. His prayer, "Lord, I desperately need you!" had opened the circuit.

As this man told me what happened, the melody and words of the gospel hymn flooded my mind and heart.

> He touched me, O, He touched me,
> and O, the joy that floods my soul;
> Something happened, and now I know,
> He touched me and made me whole. [3]

We should not be surprised when God touches a person. I've had it happen often. We should expect it when we gather for worship or are alone in the quiet of our own prayers. We all need the healing touch. The Lord is the source of all healing. When we are in need of healing spiritually, physically, emotionally, interpersonally, or in some problem of life, the Lord knows, cares, and wants to help us. The Church was meant to be a healing community and each of us is called to be an agent of healing. The healing ministry of Jesus Christ manifest so powerfully during the incarnation, is now entrusted to the Church. Prayer is our channel of power to pray for His healing in our own and others' lives.

What happened to that man as he sat in church should be anticipated and gratefully expected. In sanctuaries, doctors' offices, operating rooms, hospitals, psychiatrists' counseling rooms, and in research laboratories searching for cures to virulent disease—the divine Healer is at work. He is seeking to release His healing power.

———————————————

Great Physician, I cannot live without your touch, the supernatural intervention of Creator with creation. I lift my pain and perplexity to you today.

182

GOD'S TRANSFORMING LOVE

He Touches His Church Through Me

The indisputable origin of authentic love is in the quality of the Lord's love for us. Have we persisted in loving as He persists indefatigably with us? The love we need for others is Christ Himself invading our hearts and expressing Himself through us.

REVIVE THY CHURCH, O LORD

Where there is no vision, the people perish.
Proverbs 29:18, *KJV*

———————————————◦—————————————————

The traditional church in America faces a crisis of faith. Pastors, church officers, and many members need a penetrating renaissance in which Christ becomes the verve and vitality of a new contagion. We cannot give what we do not have nor reproduce what is not ours. The lack of enthusiasm and spontaneity in many churches has its root in "business as usual" congregational life. The challenge to discipleship is missing. Only when we dare to plan and envision what we could not do on our own strength and resources, do we need to find an intimate relationship with the Lord and become channels of

185

His impossibility-defying, momentous insight. The aching needs of our time demand it: the future of the institutional church requires it.

A study of history gives a perspective. The church has always been awakened when conditions in society are the bleakest. We are now facing seemingly insolvable problems in our national life and in international affairs. Praise God! Now is when there is a chance for the culturally conditioned institutional church to come alive and confess the subtle syncretism which has infected our life. The church is not the handmaid of culture to assume its humanly-set goals. It is the divine community of God's people, called to model life as it was meant to be. We are to be a sharp contrast, a winsome judgment, and then an agent of renaissance. The local congregation is more than a reflection of culture; it is a band of God's new breed, filled with His Spirit and equipped by the gospel to change lives and confront evil in society.

That presses us to set biblically-rooted goals for the church. Institutions, like individuals, are irrevocably in the process of becoming what they dare to envision. If we could set aside all our fears and reservations, what would be our boldest dream for the institutional church in America? Mine is for a dynamic renaissance in which the leaders and members dare to go back to basics. The need of our time is for authentic Christianity to be preached and taught, lived and shared with individuals, and for a radical, to-the-roots quality of discipleship.

And the Lord is doing it! I see it happening among denominational leaders, clergy, church officers, and congregations. We are rediscovering the basic meaning of the authentic. The rebirth of intimacy with Christ has its indisputable origin in His initiative invasion of our lives. The newfound excitement about the Lord's power is consistent with the biblical promises. What the Lord did so long ago, He is doing now. And it's congruent with reality. We are daring to listen again to the deepest needs of people and share the liberating power of the gospel to meet those aching voids. Because we are allowing the Lord to deal with our own needs, empathy is replacing aloof sympathy. A faith that was an addendum to our culturally conditioned values, is becoming the essence of a new integrated wholeness around the Lordship of Christ. The world will listen to churches like that. It's happening. A new church in America is being born!

Lord of the church, I want to be in step with the cadence of revival and renaissance which you are sounding out for your people.

LOVING
BEYOND
OUR LIMITS

Dear friends, since God so loved us, we also ought to love one another. 1 John 4:11, *NIV*

Every one of us has three things in common. We need to be loved, we need to learn how to love, and we have people in our lives who desperately need our love. The essence of life is love. Giving and receiving love. Being loved and loving is the foundation and sublime expression of authentic living. Henry Drummond was right, "Love is the greatest thing in the world." The evidence that we've had an authentic turning point is that we become recipients of a liberating love and become creative lovers of others.

Picture a scale with one bowl on each side. They are

perfectly balanced, ready for the weight to be placed on one side to be balanced by the contents of the other side.

Now on one side place Christ's love and what it means to you. Begin with His ministry as Savior and Lord. Consider how He has dealt with you just as He reached out and cared for individuals during His brief incarnation. Next contemplate His death and what that means for your forgiveness, reconciliation and freedom from guilt and self-condemnation.

Now pile onto the scale Pentecost and the Lord's return through the Holy Spirit to indwell you with power. Add to that the precious weight of His daily intervention and momentary guidance. Look at the scale tip!

Next place your own life and your efforts to love on the other side. Think about your relationships. The people whom you have tried to love and need to love. Reflect on the ones who need unmerited forgiveness and uncalculating assurance. We can hardly budge the scale to any modicum of balance. How can we ever thank the Lord enough for what He's done and does for us?

How can we ever live a life which in any way is a balance to what Christ exemplified? We can't without His indwelling Spirit. He presses us on to love in His style and by His power. The indisputable origin of authentic love is in the quality of the Lord's love for us. Have we persisted in loving as He persists indefatigably with us? The love we need for others is Christ Himself invading our hearts and expressing Himself through us. That's the secret of balancing the scale. Let Him do it!

Original love from the Lord frees us from the endless effort to please people. When we know that He is pleased with us in spite of what we've been or done, that He offers forgiveness and a million new beginnings, we can get out of the sick syndrome of trying to please the people around us. Love impels us to say and do the things people need, but not just what a whim wants. People can play us like yo-yos in an endless up and down, alternating emotional highs and lows, if we are dependent on their fluctuating emotions. Courageous loving is rooted in the constancy of Christ's love. His love never fails!

Perhaps you are in one of those slumps right now depending on people's response to you more than on the assurance of Christ's "I'll-never-let-you-go" quality of love. It happens to all of us. We can all remember times when we were hurt so badly that we questioned whether we want to try to love again.

I talked to a fellow pastor recently who confessed his anxious dependence on his congregation's approval and approbation. He said, "I'm like an actor I know who waits around by the stage door for hours, talking to people, desperately in need of being told he's great. The only difference for me is that I greet my congregation after a service anxiously awaiting the 'great sermon, you're super' responses."

The remarkable thing about this man is how much he keeps telling his people that he loves them. He's discovered that his eloquent protestation is advertising his need. He says I love you to assure the same for his people. That insecurity has taken the cutting edge out of his preaching and leadership. He avoids confrontation and adjusts his message so he will never offend. But the result was mirrored in his face. There was an equivocation in his expression, a shifting of his eyes. Solicitousness showed from his body language. Soon he became anxious, a telltale sign of suppressed anger. No longer could he say with Paul, "not as pleasing men, but God" (1 Thess. 2:4, *KJV*). It has taken a long time and penetrating fellowship with this man to recover the prophet buried in his soul.

Often we inherit the if-you-love-me-you-will-do-what-pleases-me syndrome from parents who use it as the only way to get or keep children in line. We end up playing games all through our lives.

The indwelling love of Christ makes us honest, direct, decisive. Authentic love wills the ultimate good of others and takes the initiative steps toward this end. Words and actions of love are expressed by the impelling motive power of Christ's love. We can give ourselves away recklessly for people's needs without needing them. People will know and feel they are loved. We will ring true in our relationship with them. They will know that they are valued, esteemed, cherished and that we are willing to live or die for them.

I'll never forget a visit of Frank Laubach to our home years ago. He was a man who loved profoundly. He once said, "When iron is rubbed against a magnet, it becomes magnetic. Just so, love is caught, not taught. One heart burning with love sets another on fire. The church was built on love; it proves what love can do."

Your love is a boundless waterfall and mine is often a mere trickle. Energize me, Lord of love, to follow more perfectly your model of selfless love to others.

PRAYERS THAT CARE

We constantly pray for you, that our God
may count you worthy of his calling, and
that by his power he may fulfill every good
purpose of yours and every act prompted
by your faith. 2 Thessalonians 1:11, *NIV*

The other day I received a letter of affirmation and encouragement from a man I have never met. He had heard that I was passing through a difficult period in my life because of a distressing illness in my family. The man is a recognized world leader of the Christian faith and therefore my respect for him made his letter all the more comforting. He had heard from a friend about the dark night of the soul I was experiencing.

The letter was very personal. It shared a similar experience the writer had faced and what he had learned from it. Then he told me he would pray each day for me. He said he had prayed for God to help him know how to pray for me. Then he told me specifically how God had guided him to intercede on my behalf.

192

What a boost that letter was! I felt loved and uplifted. Not only was I moved by this respected leader's concern, but because I knew of his profound prayer life, I was comforted by what God put on his heart to pray for me. The Lord was the initiator. He told the man what He was desirous of giving me so he would know what to ask for in his prayers. The letter was not only from this concerned prayer warrior, it was a message from God Himself!

Prayer is the vital vocation of the Christian. We have the privilege of sharing God's work in the world. I am convinced that our Lord has ordained that his blessing and power for us are dependent upon the prayers of others. It is as if He asked, "How much do you care? How deeply are you willing to go in your intercession? How can you ask for a costly gift for another which has cost you so little time and energy in prayer?"

I find that the greatest part of prayer for others is patient, persistent communion, and waiting for the picture of what God wants us to dare to ask. It's one thing to commit a person to God in a hasty half-minute prayer. It's something else to set aside a long period of silence. I find that it's helpful to take a clean sheet of paper and write at the top the concern which brings us to prayer for another person. Then praise God in advance for His guidance and grace; thank Him that He will use you as an agent of His intervention, then be quiet! Now trust Him to guide your writing. I am always amazed at the insight and vision I receive which I could never have produced by myself.

I am blest beneficiary of the care-filled prayers of so many Christian brothers and sisters, Lord. Use me also as an effective instrument to bless others through prayer.

ARE YOU COMMITTED TO CARING?

*There should be no division in the body, but
. . . its parts should have equal concern for
each other.* 1 Corinthians 12:25, *NIV*

The test for our inventory of our capacity to love is the extent to which we give ourselves away to people we say we love. That means the surrender to the Master of our time, schedules, priorities, money and resources. Then we need to pray for His guidance of the particular people He's placed on our personal agenda to be His love incarnate. We can't reach everyone. I experience the frustration of the immensity of human need and my limited humanity. There are not enough hours in the day to get to everyone who needs Christ's love through me. Know the feeling? The only solution is to commit each day and relate unreservedly to the people the Lord brings into our lives. He will honor our willingness to develop in-depth, caring relationships. His indwelling Spirit will give us discernment of how most creatively to give ourselves away in each relationship.

No congregation can afford enough clergy to care for a congregation. The only hope of the church is for congregations to become caring centers where people love and support each other. Often this happens when a congregation is broken down into small prayer-share-and-care groups that meet consistently during the week. Not only do people learn to support one another in the adventure of Christian living, but they become alerted to the potential power of their influence to reach more believers at work and in the community. Just think what would happen to our membership rolls if each church member singled out one person, communicated Christ's love, gave himself away lavishly, introduced the person to the new life and led him or her into church membership!

Current love keeps in contact. If we can assume that the Lord will guide us about whom He has placed on our agendas, then it is our responsibility to know what's happening in their lives. I find it helpful to make up a prayer list of the particular people the Lord has singled out for my special concern. Follow-up becomes a necessity. Letters, phone calls, visits, recreational time together, leisurely meals and spontaneous get-togethers keep me current.

People ask me, "How can you do that with all you have to do?"

My answer is, "If I am too busy to care profoundly for the people God has put on my personal agenda at this time, then I am too busy."

I believe the same is true for you. Every Christian must keep time for that special group of Christ-appointed people on his or her prayer list.

Life is short. Who are the people in your life today who need to hear words of love rooted in current understanding of what is happening to and around them? The only way to keep our relationship with the Lord vital is to grasp the opportunities to express affirming love to others. Our prayers will soon become empty and shallow if we resist the impetus of His Spirit to love.

I hear your loving call, Lord, to invest myself in the compassionate care of my family of believers. By your grace and in your strength I respond to touch your people carefully.

LOVE ME TENDER

We were gentle among you, like a mother caring for her little children.
1 Thessalonians 2:7, *NIV*

I remember a cross-Atlantic flight from London to New York on a British Airways jet. I was crammed into a no-frills economy section seat with an English engineer and a mother holding a squalling infant. The child cried incessantly for hours, upsetting all the passengers. He was hungry and the more he cried the more embarrassed the mother became. Tension bordered on pain on her face. Seated between two men, she was not about to breast-feed her distraught child. Looking back on the event, I can't imagine why the two of us were so insensitive and involved in our work that we missed what was the need of

197

this child and the frustration of his sweet young mother. I was trying to finish up some work before arriving in New York and was acting like a typical male who had forgotten how his own three children had been fed in infancy.

Finally, after hours of anguished crying, a woman British army officer came marching down the aisle of the plane with a blanket tucked under her arm. She was like one of those imposing, commanding women who have built and maintained the British Empire—broad shouldered, wide-heeled shoes, tailored uniform that made you want to salute, and the officious mannerism of a sergeant-major! Here was a kind of woman who could drive a general's command car, organize the frightened people in a bomb shelter or marshall a relief movement following a catastrophe. A special breed, indeed! She strode up with purpose in her firmly-set jaw, looking at the engineer and me with impatience and urgency. Her British accent cracked out orders to both of us. "You two—get out of there! Stop your work and move to another seat."

"Yes ma'am!" I returned, moving as fast as I could to a seat she had arranged.

Then she took the blanket and folded it around the frightened mother and her famished child.

Her voice softened as she said, "All right now, with those chaps out of the way, do what you've got to do!"

Immediately the child's crying was replaced with satisfied sounds of contentment. The whole section of the place relaxed with a smile of understanding. The tenderness of what was happening pervaded all of us, including the army officer, who tried to hide her empathy behind her crusty face.

The incident came back to me as I contemplated what Paul communicated about his love for the Thessalonians. He could not have selected a more emotional expression.

He had nursed the spiritual infants of Thessalonica with immense care. His tenderness had been given without limit to these babes in Christ as they were fed with the elemental milk of the gospel of Christ's love, forgiveness and assurance. Their turn-around had resulted in their being born again and they needed encouragement.

Tenderness is basic to all our relationships. People never outgrow their need for it. We know that from our own lives. We all need people who are for us, who understand, who listen and emphathize patiently and who enter into our joy and pain with identification and compassion. How can we give less to other people than what we constantly expect from them and our Lord?

———————————⊷━━⊶———————————

Too often, Lord, I push away loved ones with a brusque and brassy manner which mocks your standard of lovingkindness. Tenderize me, I pray! Give me a tender, winsome touch like your own.

CHRISTIANS WITH A HEALING TOUCH

Is any one of you in trouble? He should pray. Is anyone happy? Let him sing songs of praise. Is any one of you sick? He should call the elders of the church to pray over him and anoint him with oil in the name of the Lord. James 5:13,14, *NIV*

———————————◦———————————

Today we have widely divergent views of the healing ministry of the Church. There are some who are convinced that the role of the Church is to preach eternal salvation and that the care of the physical needs of people is the exclusive responsibility of the medical profession. Others preach salvation but make a major emphasis on the healing ministry. Still others emphasize healing by prayer alone and deny the use of medicine or consultation of the medical profession.

I hold what I believe is a biblical view that we are to minister to the whole person—body, mind, soul, as well as everything which concerns a person's interpersonal and social needs. We are to lead people to Christ, introduce them to the abundant life in Him, expose the secret of power in His indwelling Spirit, and help them grow in Him in every area of life. Our calling is to affirm all means of healing of the mind and body. This involves support of the medical professions and cooperative efforts to minister to the whole person.

But in addition to that, I am convinced that we are called to a specific prayer ministry for the manifold illnesses and maladies of people. This should include prayer with individuals at times of sickness, prayer groups for intercession for the sick, and public services for prayer for the spiritual, emotional, and physical needs of people. Members and friends of our congregations need an opportunity to bring their varied needs for specific prayer.

James provides guidelines for this ministry of healing. Note the many kinds of needs enumerated in the passage. There were those who were suffering who needed to pray. Others were cheerful and needed to give thanks by singing psalms to avoid pride and self-sufficiency. Then there were the sick who needed prayer for healing and anointing with oil signifying the blessing of the Spirit of the Lord. But there were also those who had fallen into sin and were in need of forgiveness.

In any congregation gathered for worship all these needs and others suggested by these categories are present in our people. There are those whose deepest need is to receive Christ as Savior and Lord of their lives. Others are facing problems in living the Christian life that need to be committed to the Lord. Still others have broken relationships which need reconciliation. Some have committed sins or known deep failure who need forgiveness and assurance of pardon. And then there are those who are distressed emotionally or under the grip of psychological problems.

Finally, there are people who are ill, facing crippling diseases, grim prognoses, and debilitating physical pain. If we really care about people, some way must be devised to give individual and specific attention to these varied diseases and distresses. A healing ministry is essential to bring people into contact and communion with the Great Physician.

In my church in Hollywood, we have followed James's admonition. The elders of the church have taken the biblical injunction seriously. They are not only the lay leaders of the spiritual life of the church and administrators of the program of the congregation, but they have been ordained to be channels of healing power through prayer for the manifold needs of the people.

This is done periodically when a major portion of the Sunday morning service is set aside for prayers for the spectrum of physical, emotional, spiritual and relational problems people are suffering. After the morning message, they gather on the chancel steps to pray with people who come forward from the congregation. After sharing their specific need they are asked to kneel and the elder lays hands on them and prays for the release of the Lord's healing power in them. People come forward seeking to know Christ, others need assurance of forgiveness, some have concerns for loved ones who are ill or troubled. Many have physical illness and still others are facing challenges where they need the Lord's guidance and strength. The results of these prayers have been astounding.

The elders are not the only people who pray for the diversity of needs. Hundreds of members of the congregation have responded to the call to a ministry of intercession. A list of the needs of people is distributed weekly to those people for daily prayers. Sensitized by the emphasis of healing prayer throughout the life of the Church, people pray for one another one to one, in small prayer groups, and over the phone. The power of God is being released through His people! The Holy Spirit gift of healing is being claimed and exercised. No one elevates himself or herself to a permanent status of being a "healer." Rather the need presented by one brings forth the gift of healing in another.

The reason that the shared ministry of healing is so crucial is that at times of need often we are unable to pray for ourselves creatively. Problems, frustrations, and physical or emotional illness debilitates our capacity to hope and pray boldly for ourselves. That's when we desperately need to be able to share our disability with a sensitive, empathetic friend who believes that the Lord is able and all that He wills is possible.

Lord of our wholeness, what a privilege to be an extension of your healing virtue through my prayers. Sensitize me today to hurting saints to whom I am called as your agent of prayerful intervention.

WHY WORRY WHEN YOU CAN PRAY?

Do not be anxious about anything, but in everything, by prayer and petition, with thanksgiving, present your requests to God. Philippians 4:6, *NIV*

———————◆———————

Focus in your mind's eye the people about whom you are concerned. The people about whom you worry. Who are they to you? Perhaps you are married to him or her. Maybe you're worried about one of your children. Or it may be a friend who's in trouble, or someone for whom you work or who works for you.

I want to share a secret of how to stop worrying about those people and start living. Intercessory prayer can break the worry bind. Worry is thinking turned toxic, concern degenerated into inner conflict. The old English word for worry is *wyrgan* which means to twist or strangle.

Worry does that to our love for people. It both twists it into debilitating anxiety and strangles our capacity to discover what to do to help and do it in a way that does not multiply the problem about which we are troubled in another person.

Worry is that anxiety which fills the interface between what is and what we imagine should be. It is the insecure, unstable fill we dump into the caverns excavated by our human expectations. It is the marshy substance that will support no bridge of safe passage; it is the aching memory of what should have been and what should be but seldom is. Worry is unproductive because it is not based on the vision of what God promises He can and will do.

Intercessory prayer is the antidote to worry over people. But many of us pray for people about whom we are concerned, and still worry.

A woman said to me recently, "I pray for my son, but can't seem to stop worrying about him. I talk to God about him and tell Him what my boy needs. But I get up from my knees and soon I am worrying as if I had never prayed."

Ever feel like that? How can we pray for people and know that God has heard us, understood, and that He will do something?

Like all prayer, intercessory prayer originates with God, not us. He has wisely decreed that His work will be done in His people cooperatively through the prayers of those on whose hearts He places His burden. If we won't pray, often He won't act. Notice I didn't say that He can't act. He can do anything He wants to do. But the mystery of His providential care of people is that He calls us into the process of His blessing, and often waits to bless a person until we pray.

The word *intercede* in the Latin means "to go or pass between"; *inter,* between; *cedere,* go on, pass. The exciting idea the Lord has been giving me is that He is the original, initiating interceder. He intercedes with us, that is, He invades our worry with specific guidance on how to pray for another person. Jesus did that for us in the incarnation and the atonement. And He continues to do that in our prayers. "He ever lives to make intercession for them" (Heb. 7:25, *NKJV*), first between us and the heart of God and then into our hearts to give the wisdom of what and how to pray for the people about whom we are tempted to worry.

But so often we worry over a person, finally decide that prayer is our last resort, and then go into God's presence to brief Him on the need and what He should do. Because we feel that it's up to us to persist and that God will bless someone because of the length and repetition of our prayers, we do not get free of the worry. We wonder, Have we said enough? Have we prayed often enough? Is our own life sufficiently in order to deserve an answer to our prayer for a loved one? Now added to our original worry is the concern about the adequacy of our prayers. We are back in the syndrome of self-justification and bartered love.

It is the Lord who calls us into prayer for people. The thought of a person's need is because He wants to act in that person's life. Part of His strategy is to involve us in His unfolding answer.

A concern for a person is a call to intercessory prayer. Worry is a substitute for intercession. And worrying after we've prayed is a sure sign that we think of prayer as our effort and that perhaps God has not heard. Added to that, it is a lack of trust. And that may tell us more about our need than the person for whom we are praying. Worry is a cycle of unproductive thought whirling around a center of hidden fear. We cannot receive the cure of our worry until we allow the Lord to show us what fear in us is causing it. Perhaps we fear losing control or want to direct another person's life. Claiming that God is in charge may be very frightening. Or we may have asked the Lord for something in our own lives and it has not come on our timing or to our specifications. We have little confidence that He will hear us in our concerns for others any more than we think He hears us about our own set of problems. Worry is the natural result of unbelief.

The problem is that worry becomes a habit. After a while, we need it to feel secure. We are like dope addicts needing a fix. We can actually create situations about which we can worry. What can we do? The cure of worry is not just the belief that things will work out for good under the providence of God. It comes from wrenching our egos from the throne of our hearts. Worry is a manifestation that we are still living with our wills in control and our desires as the focus of our prayers. The worry syndrome is seldom broken until we are willing to be called into prayer to receive God's orders for what is best rather than tenaciously grasping what we are determined to convince Him should be done.

Theologian and author Helmut Thielicke said, "Care can be cured only by care. Care about many things can be cured only by care about the one thing needful. This is the homeopathy of divine healing."

And the one thing needful? Jesus said it was to seek first God's kingdom and all else would be given. The creative fear of missing the reason we were born displaces all secondary fears. When we put God first in our lives, people and their needs become a close second. The ministry of prayer is not an option for those so inclined by nature. Our new nature in Christ is manifested in the willingness to be called by Him into a ministry of listening for what we are to pray for others, and then responding by asking with boldness for those things He has clarified.

The issue raised about intercessory prayer is whether our prayers for others make any difference. Often we ask: Can our prayers change God's will for a person? Can our sincere wish alter the counsel of the Almighty? What I have tried to communicate here is that those questions indicate we are missing the purpose of intercessory prayer.

The real question is: Can God implant in our minds the maximum expression of His will for another person? Can we cooperate with Him in the accomplishment of His will by praying for him or her?

Yes! And when we receive that and respond in our prayers, we become essential agents for the Lord to pour out His blessings. Oneness with Him and the persons for whom we pray will result. We can stop worrying and start living!

———————◦———————◦———————

What joy to stand in the gap for others, Lord! I stand ready to be a prayer bridge linking you and your loved ones.

WHEN GOD CLEANS HOUSE

The Son of Man will send out his angels,
and they will weed out of his kingdom
everything that causes sin and all who do
evil. Matthew 13:41, *NIV*

S ome time ago, I had the questionable notoriety of
being listed as one of the 10 most dangerous leaders
of the Church in America. My vision for the renewal
of the Church ran counter to the ideas of the author of the
list. I gained some comfort in the fact that my friend Billy
Graham was also listed, along with eight others whom I
love and admire. The listmaker's purge of the leadership of
the Church was not taken seriously, and soon was publicly
repudiated as one more of his vitriolic pronouncements.

The title of the list lingered in my mind for a long time

and led to a profound question: Who are the really dangerous people in the Church? Or, to put it more personally:
Who are the dangerous people in your congregation and
mine? Our minds leap immediately to the people with
whom we may not agree on a particular policy or whose
priorities are different from ours. But go deeper. Every
congregation has a group of dangerous people. Dangerous
not to us and our ambitions, but to our Lord. Before we
list them, be careful. We may be among them ourselves.

The local congregation is made up of two kinds of people. It makes all the difference for now and eternity which
group we're in. The great challenge is to liberate people
from one category to the other.

The Church of Jesus Christ is made up of inside-
outsiders and inside-insiders. The first group makes up
the most dangerous people in the Church. Only two people have the prerogative of determining which group
you're in—Jesus Christ and you.

The insider-outsider and the inside-insider often look
alike, sound similar and both believe in Jesus Christ. Their
relationship to Him as Lord couldn't be more dissimilar.
What's the difference?

The inside-outsider is in the Church but outside a
deep, intimate relationship with Christ. He believes that
Jesus Christ is the Savior of the world but has never come
to know Him as the Lord of his life. There never has been
a time of complete commitment of all he has and is. The
power of the Christian life is experienced in daily, specific
surrender of the needs, challenges, problems and opportunities of life. The inside-outsider is inside the Church,
but outside of an intimate, impelling, indwelling experience
of Christ as Lord.

One of the most gratifying and puzzling phenomena of
our time is the great number of church members who are

discovering the joy and freedom of committing their lives to Christ. They are discovering the excitement of trusting Christ with their frustrations and fears.

Recently, a church member realized the power of Christ in his life. At a party of fellow members, he shared the delight of his experience. It was very disturbing to some when he said, "I've been a Presbyterian for years. Last week I found out what it's all about to be a Christian. I've always believed that Christ was Savior, but for the first time I know He's my Savior! It's alarming to think of all the joy I've missed being an uncommitted church member. Now I know Christ as the Lord of all my relationships and responsibilities."

Perhaps it was the fact that this man had been a church officer, generous giver and leader of the church which contributed to the wonderment of his friends. But most of all, it made them wonder about themselves. Was there something missing in their lives?

This church member had become an inside-insider: inside the Church and inside a personal relationship with Christ. He was no longer running his own life. Christ had taken charge as Lord. Previously Christ and the Church had been two of the many loyalties and concerns of his busy life. But he was in control. He seldom prayed, except in crises. His own sagacity and strength were the source of his clever life. His plans were always within the limits of his own power and ability. The decisions he made at his office and on a church board were marked by caution, concern and dependence on human skill and adequacy. His family was filled with stress and he was disturbed when his children did not adopt his bland mixture of moralism and regulations.

Most of all, my friend was tense and tight until he became an inside-insider. As long as he remained the lord

211

of his own life, he continued to have problems and be a problem.

He was one of the most dangerous men in his church. Why? Because his pretentious facsimile looked like the real thing. And he kept his church locked on dead center. He would not allow his church to move beyond what he had experienced. He was a stumbling block to progress.

There is no more crucial issue before the Church today than how to make inside-insiders out of inside-outsiders. It's never easy. Inside-outsiders think they have experienced all that there is to be discovered in the Christian life. They are dangerous because they want to do God's work in their own strength. It won't work!

Billy Graham is often criticized because so many of his converts are church members. That says a lot more about the local congregation in America than it does about the Graham crusades. Hundreds of thousands of inside-outsiders who are members of churches have discovered the liberation of a personal commitment to Christ at the crusades.

Some time ago I completed a series of meetings in a church in Arkansas. On the last evening I asked those who wanted to surrender complete control of their lives to Christ for the first time to stand. I was amazed at the large number of church members who stood up. One man said, "I've been waiting for 66 years to hear what you said about commitment tonight and to respond. Thanks for not taking us for granted."

There is a great movement mounting in our day. It is made up of people who are discovering that there is more to Christianity than acceptance of Christ. They are experiencing the energizing, liberating power of surrendering all they know of themselves to however much they know of Christ. The most dangerous people in the church are becoming the most dynamic. There is little distinction in believing in Jesus as the Savior of the world. The devil believes that! The power, peace and triumph of the Christian life is available when Christ takes up residence and reigns on the throne of our hearts.

Holy Lord, move in power through your Church, purifying her to authentic sainthood. Here I am—begin with me!

GOD'S TRANSFORMING LOVE

He Reaches His World Through Me

It is every Christian's birthright to be a reproducer.
The untapped reservoir for the evangelization
of the world is the contagious believer.
Our challenge is to discover a winsome way of
sharing our faith that works for us.

LIFE'S GREATEST TURNAROUND

You turned to God from idols to serve the
living and true God.
1 Thessalonians 1:9, *NIV*

———————◇——┊——◇———————

As I drove a rented car in a strange city searching for
a church where I was to speak, I suddenly realized I
had passed the address and was heading in the
wrong direction. I tried to turn around but each intersec-
tion had a large "No U-Turn" sign. Irritated, I finally
turned off the thoroughfare and headed down a side street
hoping to be able to double back. It was a cul-de-sac with a
large traffic sign which read just the opposite of the ones
which had kept me moving away from my destination. This
one, obviously painted by residents who wanted to main-
tain the privacy of their dead-end street, boldly pro-

217

claimed, "U-Turn Absolutely Required!" My frustration was replaced with delight. I had experienced a contemporary parable.

The Christian life begins with an authentic conversion. The word "conversion" means to turn around. A U-turn is absolutely required. Rather than running away from God in willful independence, we can turn around and move toward Him in response to His outstretched arms of love, forgiveness, grace and peace. An authentic conversion is of undisputed origin, genuine, trustworthy, certain, current, verifiable, true and sure. A decisive U-turn is in response to God's call. It is a real about-face; it changes the total direction of our lives and stands the test of time.

The great need today is for the conversion of religious people who, though they believe in God, are heading away from Him and not to Him. Many church people are trying to live a life they have never begun. I said that at a conference of church leaders recently. I was surprised, and then alarmed, by how many agreed. Some told me of their own traumatic conversions after some years in the church and the ministry. Others shared the stories of members of their churches who were completely turned around through a personal, fresh experience of God's grace and a complete surrender of their lives to His guidance and power.

The most satisfying thing I see happening today in the new renaissance in the church is that people who had drifted into the church with a vague half-belief, are experiencing an authentic conversion. Beyond a genealized hunch, they are finding hope; more than ideas about God, they are discovering intimacy with Him; instead of running away from God, they are allowing Him to run their lives. The authentic is replacing the apocryphal. A new church is being born in our time! It is made up of soundly converted people who have made a U-turn that is genuine.

An authentic conversion will result in the conversion of others. It is safe to say that we have not experienced a U-turn unless we can identify people we have influenced for Christ by our witness, and helped them through the steps of conversion. All the techniques of evangelism, devised with mass meetings and programs, will never substitute for the one-to-one influence on others which the radically converted Christian exerts. It is every Christian's birthright to be a reproducer. The untapped reservoir for the evangelization of the world is the contagious believer. Our challenge is to discover a winsome way of sharing our faith that works for us.

I am convinced that if each of us lived our faith with "all-stops-out" enthusiasm, and were willing to talk about what Christ means to us in the pressures of life, we would have more opportunities to help others find a personal relationship with Christ than we ever imagined.

In communicating the faith, utilize these nine crucial steps:

1. Help people know that they are elected, called, chosen. No one longs to find God who has not first been found by Him.

2. Explain the simple promises of the gospel with the confidence that the Holy Spirit is at work in minds and hearts creating receptivity and openness. Tell them God loves them. Share the profound meaning of the cross for their forgiveness and reconciliation. Communicate the secret that to love God is to allow Him to love them.

3. Assure them that God's love will never let them go. They belong to Him, now and for eternity.

4. Enable them to accept the gift of faith from the Holy

219

Spirit to appropriate all that was done for them on Calvary and surrender all of the past, present and future to Him.

5. Affirm the new love for God, self and others which begins to flow in a person as the evidence that the Lord has taken up residence in him or her. Help the new convert to be to others what Christ has been to him or her. Help the person do a relational inventory. Whom does he need to forgive; whose forgiveness should he seek? What restitution for past sin needs to be done? Love wipes the slate clean so we can live with freedom.

6. Show from your own life how hope in Christ has worked for you and can work for him or her in all of life's challenges and opportunities. Encourage the person to commit all the uncertainties and problems to Him, expecting His intervention.

7. Stay in touch with the person until he or she becomes a follower of the Lord. That means discovering the power of prayer for guidance in all of life's decisions and needs. An intimate companionship with the Master is the essence of the Christian life.

8. Encourage the joy the Lord gives in affliction. It will come as the person sorts out the implications of obedience to Christ. Help maximize the joy the Lord provides in the times of testing. Be an encourager.

9. Become a strategist in helping the person discover the power of his or her influence. Our work is not finished until the person has led another person to Christ. Help him to become aware of people's need for what has happened to him. We can keep only what we give away! You will have helped a person live life as it was meant to be.

If we are to cooperate with what God wants to do, a U-turn is absolutely required—in each of us and then through us in others. Everything else the Lord longs to give us is dependent on a complete turn-around, an authentic conversion.

———————————◆—————————————

Lord of life, I submit myself ever to be a warm and winsome turn-around standard directing a hurting world back to you.

ARE YOU A GOOD NEWS STORY?

I am not ashamed of the gospel, because it is the power of God for the salvation of everyone who believes. Romans 1:16, *NIV*

———— ◇———:———◇ ————

I stood outside an auditorium waitng to be introduced to preach. An outstanding, elderly, evangelical scholar, whom I respect very much, came up to me with a moving challenge. "Give us the gospel according to Lloyd!"

I must have shown shock on my face at this startling admonition. The brilliant, seasoned saint went on to explain: "We want to hear what Christ means to you; the difference He has made in your life; the way the biblical truth is enabling you to cope with the tough issues today.

Give us the distilled essence of your gospel passed through the fires of experience."

As I waited, reflecting on that, my mind drifted back to some favorite words spoken long ago by Bishop William Alfred Quayle, the American Methodist bishop (1860-1925). They are equally applicable to the witness of the laity or clergy. "Preaching is the art of making a sermon and delivering that. Why no, that is not preaching. Preaching is the art of making a preacher, and delivering that. Preaching is the outrush of soul in speech. Therefore the elemental business in preaching is not with the preaching but with the preacher. It is no trouble to preach, but a vast trouble to construct a preacher. What, then, in the light of this is the task of a preacher? (Or of anyone sharing his or her faith.) Mainly this, the amassing of a great soul so as to have something worthwhile to give—the sermon is the preacher up to date."

The word "gospel" means good news. The word in Greek, *euaggelion,* had three uses in ancient times: It meant the bearer of good news, the good news itself, and the reward given to the bearer of the good news. All three have meaning for us. We are the communicators of the good news of the life, message, death, reconciliation and resurrection of Jesus Christ. What He accomplished for our salvation, eternal life and abundant living is the content of our good news. He, Himself, is our reward.

The gospel contains the truth of what Christ did and does. It is the declaration of the promise of life as it was meant to be. The content of the gospel is the message of the New Testament. It is to become my gospel and your gospel. The gospel according to you and me is the gospel which has been ingrained into our thinking, understanding, action and attitude. Biblical truth passed through the tempering of experience until it is an integrated part of us. We

223

are not only to believe the good news, but are to be good news incarnate. The gospel on two legs walking. Only "our" gospel can sustain us in a time like this.

———————◇———◇———◇———

How important it is, Lord, that when my neighbors scan the pages of my life they clearly read your story. May I be a transparent transmitter of the gospel today!

HOW TO REALLY SUCCEED IN LIFE?

*He is like a tree planted by streams of
water, . . . whatever he does prospers.*
Psalms 1:3, *NIV*

———◇—◆—◇———

S uccess has become a dirty word in some Christian
circles. We look down our noses at successful people. Often when describing what a person was before
conversion we allude to his worldly success as if the new
life in Christ will now make him a worldly loser.

Is the Lord against success? Doesn't He want us to
use our gifts, multiply our resources and maximize our
opportunities? Why are we critical of successful people?
What is this love-hate implication we give when we condemn prosperity all through the year and go to the prosperous at stewardship time to collect the results of their

industry? We honor successful entertainers and leaders, and at the same time give the impression that if they really loved Jesus they would sell all and go into the professional ministry. Is there anything wrong with being successful?

We must define our terms. Success is the favorable or prosperous course or accomplishment of anything attempted. The word implies the result or outcome of a plan, purpose or effort. A successful person is one who obtains what he desires or intends. He accomplishes what he sets out to do.

Those definitions are benign enough. There is nothing wrong in fulfilling a purpose or in accomplishing a goal. The crucial issue is the nature of the desired end. True success is measured by that.

Some of us have made success itself our god. We can deify our ideas of prosperity and miss the relationship with the true God. The Lord God who is Creator, Sustainer and Redeemer of the world does want us to be successful— but according to His goals, plan and design. The authentically successful have Him and His will as the measurement of their success.

Look at it this way. God had a purpose in the creation of the universe. He has been moving toward the accomplishment of that purpose throughout history. On this planet He created plant, animal and human levels of life. He created man to love Him and receive His love. He gave us the wondrous gift of free will so that we could choose to love Him and cooperate with Him. His intention for us was sublime companionship. But when we rebelled, He was not outdone. He came to us Himself to expose His nature and reveal His ultimate purpose for His people. The Lord dwelt among us full of grace and truth. He lived, died and was raised up so that our sin of separation and rebellion could be forgiven.

The same creative Spirit who made us, who came to save us, and who defeated the power of sin and death, continues with us. His post-Pentecost home is our forgiven and receptive hearts. From within us, He calls us to work wtih Him in making our lives, our relationships and our world what He intended them to be. Jesus said that we were to be perfect (*telos*) as God is perfect. The word *telos* in Greek means "end, goal or purpose; to accomplish that end or purpose."

Success, then, is cooperating with God in establishing the Kingdom of God in our hearts, all of our affairs, our personal relationships, and our society. Whatever else we accomplish during the years of our life, however much we accumulate or acquire, unless we discover a personal relationship with Christ, seek to do His will in all of life and test everything according to His purpose, we will not be successful. Right at this moment God wants to make us successful—on His terms, by His power, and on His timing. He is the God of the successful.

My friends Geoff and Betty Kitson led what they called a "workshop for worriers" at a conference. God has given these two adventurers a secret to unlock worry. Their lives were committed to "barn building" until they both discovered true wealth in Jesus Christ. Now what they have is poured out for people. Betty is deeply involved in helping children with remedial reading. Geoff has come out of a secure retirement to communicate Christ to individuals as the leader of the Faith at Work movement.

Over dinner the other evening, my wife and I were deeply moved by the vitality and viability of these two contagious people. God is using them mightily. They are succeeding on God's terms. All the drive, ambition and creativity they have is invested in the Kingdom business.

God is the God of the successful. When we give Him

our lives, relinquish control of our possessions, seek His will in all things, we will succeed. As someone said aptly, "God don't make no failures—He helps them!" and I say He helps them succeed on His terms and for His glory.

I want to be successful, Lord, but only on your terms. May the Kingdom of God advance in the world today because of me, not in spite of me.

THE WORK OF WITNESSING

Whatever you do, work at it with all your heart, as working for the Lord, not for men.
Colossians 3:23, *NIV*

The person in Christ is to be distinguished for his conscientious, industrious integrity. The Lord is our true Master. We are to do our work as if we were working for Him. Some years ago, I had an assistant who worked harder than any pastor I have ever known. He was tireless in his efforts to do everything I suggested, and then so much more beyond. One day I said to him in appreciation, "I am deeply gratified by how hard you work for me."

He smiled and then said, "Thanks for saying that. But you know, I really am not doing it for you, but for the Lord!" Paul would have liked that answer.

When our work is done "as to the Lord" (Col. 3:23, *KJV*), it takes on a new perspective, as well as a new excellence. At the end of each day or project, we should be able to say, "Lord, I've done my best because I did it for you." We have no other purpose than to please the Lord.

But that's not always true. Remuneration, recognition, false pride, competitiveness and compulsion often are our motives. We need to ask, "Why am I doing what I do?" The fact is that we were never meant to find meaning in our work, but rather bring meaning to our work. When Christ is our meaning we can work creatively to praise Him. When our work becomes too important we make it a false god. That can be true whether we work on an assembly line or in the pulpit. Some of us have confused our self-worth with overwork. We feel urged to justify ourselves with our own performances. True freedom in our employment comes when we seek the Lord's guidance about where to work, ask Him for His strength to work industriously and effectively, and leave the results of our success to Him.

When we place ourselves under the leadership of an employer we are to be obedient to that person as an act of faithfulness to Christ.

There are times when it's difficult to work for people whose purposes and goals, along with their policies and practices, contradict our convictions. Often our prayers lead us to change employment, but not before we have done all we can to share Christ and what He means to us with the people for whom we work. I believe that the Lord plants us in these very places where the gospel is needed most. Our reason for being there is not just for the job, but also for what the Lord wants to have happen to the people with whom He has put us in contact.

I know a young lawyer who has claimed the floor of the office building in which he works for Christ. The Lord has put him into contact with many people who need faith and hope.

A woman who works in a department store said, "I couldn't take working in here if it weren't for the chance to pray for the people I wait on."

An insurance man sees his work with people as an opportunity to share Christ's eternal life policy. And so it goes. Saints in the marketplace, alive in Christ, using the relationships at work to spread the gospel.

***

Somehow, Lord, the love and devotion for you which saturates my Sunday worship needs to stream through my workday world. Help me be a seven-day saint, captivating co-workers with a faith that works.

THE BENEFITS
OF BEING
A SALTY SAINT

You are the salt of the earth. But if the salt loses its saltiness, how can it be made salty again? It is no longer good for anything, except to be thrown out and trampled by men. Matthew 5:13, *NIV*

A young lad whose excitement for sports outdistanced his devotion to studies, brought home his report card. He put off showing it to his parents as long as he could. Finally, the moment of truth could be avoided no longer. His parents read the grades with concern, but not surprise. Then they read his teacher's comments in the report: "Johnny does well at school, but he could do much better if the sheer joy of living didn't impede his progress!"

I can picture Johnny in that classroom, wriggling and waiting for recess or the time for play at the end of the afternoon. At that stage of his life being a pitcher was more important than algebra or the facts of history.

We smile, and remember how it felt. Then we reflect

on the teacher's analysis. Not true! The joy of living never impeded anyone's progress. It inspires it.

Someone asked me what I wanted for my life and the people I love. The words of Johnny's teacher came to mind. I long for all of us to experience the sheer joy of living.

So does Jesus. Jesus came to enable Christians with a tang—distinctive, sharp, pungent. Salty Christians with an incisive quality that seasons the life of others and society. Saline saints bring zest and gusto to life. Like salt, they bring out the best of the flavor of living.

The secret of the Christian life is in its impossibility. It was never meant to be lived on our own wisdom or power. A Christian with tang is one who dares to believe that, because the Lord is present, there is no limit to the miraculous interventions of His power that can invade the impotence of our daily lives. We salt life with a vibrant expectation.

When everyone else is negative and cautious, a salty Christian asks only two questions: "What does the Lord want?" and "How can we receive the unlimited resources of His power?" A person with that kind of expectancy will flavor the dull gruel of depleted human potential. Every person, family, and church needs people who have not lost the savor of a bold belief in the possibilities the Lord is ready to unleash.

The other evening I arrived at church to lead a Sunday evening service completely exhausted. Before the service, I had a deep time of fellowship and prayer with my elders. They discerned the source of the energy drain in worry over an impossible load of detail and uncompleted tasks in preparation for the new program year. I had begun to take the whole responsibility on myself. Grimness and self-doubt invaded my mind. When they prayed, laying hands on me, I felt a new freedom to let go of my control and receive the Holy Spirit for the burdens. After prayer we all went into the sanctuary to lead a communion and healing service. The Lord answered the elders' prayers. I felt new energy, and excitement begin to flow again.

The world desperately needs energetic Christians with a lively verve for life. But we cannot give what we do not have. Only the Lord can refurbish enthusiasm.

Coupled with enthusiasm is humor. Christians are not noted for their humor. Robert Louis Stevenson returned from church and was delighted to say, "I've been to church and I am not depressed."

All too often church and church people are depressing because they have lost the tang of laughing at themselves. Our Lord wants to liberate overly grim, uptight Christians. His forgiveness should make us much more tender on ourselves and others. It frees us to share and laugh with others over our mistakes and blunders. Then the people around us are free to accept their own humorous humanity. A sure sign that we have become salty saints is in the quality and quantity of our humor.

Rufus Mosley was once asked, "Did Jesus laugh?"

His response was, "I don't know, but He sure fixed me up so that I could!"

So say I.

The sheer joy of living! We have been called to be Christians with a tang. There's a new image of life for our imagination. What would it be like for you today to be the Lord's flavor, seasoning and zest?

Sprinkle me generously, Lord, into my bland environment to be that zesty zing which makes people hungry for you.

234

THERE'S STILL TIME FOR TELLING

I tell you, now is the time of God's favor,
now is the day of salvation.
2 Corinthians 6:2, *NIV*

Two questions must be asked and answered by each of us. One is very personal, and the other may seem presumptuous at first. How old are you? What time of the day is it for your life?

I am indebted to Leslie Weatherhead for his tabulation of our age and the hours of a day. For some it's early in the day of life; for others close to midnight. Find yourself in this chart. Weatherhead says,

> Take the measure of the years by reducing a lifetime of seventy years to the compass of the

235

waking hours of a single day from, say, seven in the morning till eleven at night. Then if you are:

15 years of age, the time is 10:25 A.M.
20 years of age, the time is 11:34 A.M.
25 years of age, the time is 12:42 P.M.
30 years of age, the time is 1:51 P.M.
35 years of age, the time is 3:00 P.M.
40 years of age, the time is 4:08 P.M.
45 years of age, the time is 5:16 P.M.
50 years of age, the time is 6:25 P.M.
55 years of age, the time is 7:34 P.M.
60 years of age, the time is 8:42 P.M.
65 years of age, the time is 9:51 P.M.
70 years of age, the time is 11:00 P.M.[1]

This helps us identify where we are in the adventure of living.

Once I had the privilege of introducing an old man and a teenage woman to Christ in the same week. A young woman by the name of Beth is now filled with the joy and peace of Christ. She is excited about a full life ahead of growing in the Savior. She entered the vineyard very early.

The elderly man was close to the end of his life. His energies are spent; all he had to bring to the Lord was a long life of regrets. His whole life had been spent on himself and his own desires. The plow of self-concern had cut deep furrows on his brow and lines on his face. Now sickness had brought him to the realization of his desperate need for God. He was not ready to die. He feared the judgment of God. Then, as he repeated the sinner's prayer after me, I sensed the presence of the loving Lord.

Afterward he said, "How I wish I hadn't waited so

236

long. There's not much time left to enjoy my new life."

I assured him he had all of eternity.

Neither the young woman nor the old man was called and chosen because of what he or she had or had not done. The reward was the same for both.

We put so much emphasis on when people respond to God. In evangelism we spend a great deal of time and effort trying to create the right atmosphere, have the best music, and set the most inviting mood. We forget that faith is a gift, and no one can respond to his or her election without the gift from the Spirit of God. Our only concern is to make the love of God clear, explain the gospel impellingly, and invite people to respond winsomely. If we care for them personally and God has worked in their hearts, they will respond. The glory will not be given to our effective methods, but to God.

To labor with the Lord, long or short, is the blessing which is ours by grace. There's a sixteenth-century prayer which articulates the joy of that. "Teach us to labor and not to ask for any reward save that of knowing that we do Thy will." Thomas Aquinas knew the essence of that. One time he heard the Lord say to him in a dream, "Thomas, thou hast written much and well concerning me. What reward shall I give thee for thy work?"

Thomas' reply was, "Nothing but Thyself, Lord!"

Companionship with the Lord is the ultimate reward. We are free to love God for God, not because of what He will do for us or we have done for Him.

I heard one of the elders of our church pray, "Thank you, Lord, that you called me on my mother's knee and helped me to know you as a child so that I could enjoy you all through the years."

If you can say that, praise God. But if it's the noon hour of your life, the invitation is open. And if it's the last hour, it's not too late. A companionship that death cannot end can begin right now.

Lord of my minutes, days and years, I'm grateful for those who sensed the urgency of my need of salvation. May I respond in kind to people around me of every age.

ARE YOU A FRUITFUL FOLLOWER?

I am the vine; you are the branches. If a man remans in me and I in him, he will bear much fruit; apart from me you can do nothing. John 15:5, *NIV*

What measurements would you use to evaluate the effectiveness of a church? What would you say distinguishes a great congregation?

Many of us think of the local church as an end in itself. Therefore, our answers about the success of a church would be to judge what happens within the building and program of the congregation. The size of the membership, the quality of the preaching, the vitality of the edcucational program or the warmth of the fellowship would be our measuring lines. We think of the church as something we go to for inspiration, enrichment and encouragement.

These are all crucial elements of a dynamic church, but are not the ultimate test of greatness.

The church is not only a place we go; it is what we are between Sundays. It is the equipping center for the ministry of the laity in the world. The effectiveness of worship, education and fellowship has a bottomline accountability in the quality of people the congregation produces for discipleship in daily living.

The one test of a great church is the fruitfulness of its people. The congregation exists to produce fruitful followers of Christ.

We are to abide in Christ and invite Him to abide in us. When we abide in Christ, we appropriate all He has done for us. That means unreserved acceptance of His death for our sins and His resurrection for the defeat of all the enemies of the abundant life. The Greek word for abide is *meno*. It is drenched with meaning. To abide means to dwell, remain, and rest. The word also implies to continue in a relationship, faithful and unchanging. Sojourn, tarry and wait are synonymous for abide. Most of all, it means to remain continuously. We abide in Christ when we accept His love as our assurance, His forgiveness as our freedom, and His presence as our power. Fruitfulness has no beginning if it does not begin by abiding—trusting completely in Christ for our salvation and our eternal life.

But that's only the beginning. We were created for Christ to abide in us. He is the indwelling Lord in the contemporary power of the Holy Spirit. When we commit our lives to Him, we become the post-Pentecost abiding, dwelling place of the Lord. That's the secret of fruitfulness. From within, He begins His transforming work.

The apostle John clarifies that in his first epistle to the churches. He writes to assure the Christians that they have been born of God because God's seed abides in them (see 1 John 3:9). We are the begotten of God, chosen to be reformed in the image of Christ. Through the seed of Christ in us, God's nature, revealed in Jesus, is reproduced in us. That means that our thought, temperament, and disposition are being remolded in Christ-likeness. The progression is exciting: we are born of God, chosen and called. We abide in His love for us in Christ, and then He abides in us for the transformation of our character. The fruit of Christ indwelling is the new you and I, recreated as new creatures in Christ.

Fruitfulness also is expressed through our personality. That's what Paul meant when he talked about the fruit of the Spirit. Christ's Spirit, abiding in us, manifests the character of Christ through us. Here then is personal fruitfulness as the result of Christ making us like Himself: love, joy, peace, patience, kindness, goodness, faithfulness, gentleness and self-control (see Gal. 5:22). These are the figs the Lord wants to grow on the tree of our lives. None is available, apart from Him. We can inventory our fruitfulness by evaluating the evidence of the fruit of His Spirit. But catch the wonder of it all: the fruit our Lord demands He imputes as His gift.

That presses us on to the fruit He wants to produce through us with others. It's summarized in the Lord's commandment, "This is My commandment, that you love one another, just as I have loved you" (John 15:12, *NASB*).

How has he loved us? The next verse answers our question. "Greater love has no one than this, that one lay down his life for his friends" (v. 13). There it is! Fruitfulness is loving people as we have been loved with giving, forgiving, sacrificial love. The test of fruitfulness is laying down our lives for others.

It meant Calvary for Christ. For us it means vulnerability, openness, and involvement with people. If we love

241

people, we will want them to know the joy we have found. Fruitfulness is the sharing of our faith with others and introducing them to the love of Christ. Unwillingness to help others find Christ is not shyness; it is lack of love. It is as if we had discovered a cure for a form of cancer we are suffering and being unwilling to share our gift of healing.

Can you imagine refusing to communicate our healing if it could help other sufferers? And yet, one of the greatest problems in the local church today is to liberate the dumbness of contemporary Christians about what Christ has done for them. There are church members who have occupied pews for years and can account for not one person whom they have helped live forever!

The apostle John knew no such reticence. "Again I say, we are telling you about what we ourselves have actually seen and heard, so that you may share the fellowship and the joys we have with the Father and with Jesus Christ his Son" (1 John 1:3, *TLB*).

Reproduction of our faith in others is the test of fruitfulness. We are productive trees in the Lord's vineyard if we have the figs of hope for people. We lay down our lives when we crucify our privation, separateness, and lack of concern. The Lord constantly sends us people to look for life through us. Many of them are as disappointed as He was when He went to the fig tree looking for fruit.

That was not true for a new-members class that joined our church in Hollywood recently. I can still feel the thrill I had when I looked over the faces of the 45 candidates for baptism and membership in the Body of Christ. The exciting thing about this class was that most of the people had been introduced to Christ and the church by members of the congregation. They had been loved, listened to, cared for and witnessed to by fruitful contemporary disciples.

242

Joy filled the sanctuary as those members saw the tangible fruit of their ministry. There were people in the class from all walks of life. Each had been alerted to what was missing in his or her life by members whose character and personality radiated with Christ's indwelling power. Executives, professors, movie personalities, students, housewives, singles, couples, youth and adults all had been initiated to the abundant life by people in whom the fruit of the Spirit abounded.

As I received the class into membership and commissioned them to be fruitful disciples in their ministry, I was very aware that the new Christians would be able to grow in what they had discovered only as they too became fruitful. Christ's abiding presence would enable that. He will transform their natures to be like His own. Then He will expect reproduction of new life in others.

One of our deacons confessed, "I sat in this church for 20 years before I took seriously what I heard and began to be a fruitful Christian. I hate to think about all I missed during those years!" He is a part of a breed of articulate, contagious Christians who now measure their spiritual life on their effectiveness at multiplying the new life in others.

The only hope for our church or any church being great will be in the extent of the fruitfulness of the members. It's the one test of a great church.

You, Lord, are the nourishing vine, my life blood, my only eternal source. Find in me today unrestricted passage resulting in abundant fruitfulness in my tasks and relationships.

OUR STORY HAS A HAPPY ENDING

For the Lord himself will come down from heaven, with a loud command, with the voice of the archangel and with the trumpet call of God . . . Therefore encourage each other with these words.
1 Thessalonians 4:16,18, *NIV*

———————◦———◦———————

The man at the next table in a restaurant where I was having breakfast punctuated his reading of the morning paper with deep groans of discouragement. Each page of the current national and international news brought a more profound sigh expressing the man's frustration with the world.

A lovely young waitress became concerned as she poured him another cup of coffee. "Is everything all right, sir?" she inquired with alarm. "You seem to be very upset about something."

"You bet I am! Haven't you read the morning paper?

244

I'm sick to death of all the bad news," he replied with consternation.

"You've got to have hope!" the young woman said timidly.

The man's response was a classic. Anger mingled with frustration. The question he asked the waitress is on everyone's hearts these days. "Hope? How can you have hope in a world like this?"

How would you have answered this pessimist? I turned to him and picked up on the wording of his question. "I don't have hope in our world, but I have hope in the world," I said, purposely playing on the words.

"Now what do you mean by that?!" was his anticipated response. I moved over to his table for my second cup of coffee, grasping the serendipity the Lord had arranged.

I tried to explain that the one thing the world could not provide is hope. Hope is elusive: you can never find it by searching for it. It is inadvertent, coming from something else. The world—possibilities, people, progress—are all unreliable sources of hope. They always let us down. The reason for the virulent hopelessness of our time is that it has finally dawned on us that no leader, negotiated peace, armed might, or human cleverness can bring the utopia we've believed was the goal of history. The only way we can live with confidence in any period of history is to have an ultimate conviction about what will happen at the end of history. Where is it all leading? Only a hope that covers all the exigencies of God's plan and purpose for history will sustain us in this turbulent phase of history.

Emil Brunner, Swiss theologian, said, "What oxygen is for the lungs, such is hope for the meaning of life." The spiritual asphyxiation of our time is the result of a profound lack of hope. The false gods of our inadequate hoping have fallen from their thrones. We've lost the idea that everything will eventually work out; that given time, we can solve the soul-sized problems which beset us. And I say: Thank God! The disillusionment of our times is the raw material of a new receptivity in all of us in which authentic hope can be born.

Authentic hope must have an ultimately reliable source, sustain us in all of life's circumstances, and answer all of our questions about present times in the light of the end times. Only Jesus Christ can give that kind of authentic hope. Consistent, lasting hope is a relational dynamic which comes from a personal, intimate trust in the One who came, comes, and is coming. All three dimensions are required for a liberating hope. One without the other, or especially the first two without the last, will leave us unprepared to deal with the questions and quandaries of life today.

Some of us are clear about the Christ who came but are uncertain about how He intervenes in our needs today. Others are sure about what He did and does, but are very unsure about what He will do when He returns, not only as Lord of life, but ultimately as Lord of history as we know it. The lack of clear preaching and teaching about the Second Coming and the end times have left us without authentic Christian hope.

Allow your mind to linger on that momentous event. Picture Christ, the company of heaven, loved ones who have gone on to heaven, all participating in the victorious intervention. Christians here on earth will be called to join them and together we will all share in worshipping. What will it be like? Human rhetoric is inadequate to describe it. All we know is that when we are liberated from the limitations of this life, we will be able to know Christ as He is and we will be known as we are. We will give Him unfettered praise and adoration and we will enjoy unencum-

246

bered fellowship of the saints with Christ. What more do we need to know? The Christ who came, comes daily, is coming. Are we ready, expectant?

We come back to my breakfast friend's question. How can we have hope in a world like this? We can't! Our hope is not in the world or in our efforts to bring the kingdom on earth, but in the Lord Christ who came, comes and is coming. I'm happy to report that my time that morning in the restaurant began a great, new friendship. Subsequently, the man gave his life to Christ and put on the breastplate of faith and love plus the helmet of hope. He's now alive forever. When his physical death comes, it will not be anything more than passing from stage of eternal life to the next. If the end of the world comes before or after his physical death, he won't miss either the rapture or the millennium or an endless life in glory after that.

Do you have that assurance? Why not live today as if it were the last day? What would you do? What would you settle in your relationship with the Lord?

———◇⇒◆⇐———

Lord and Blessed Hope, I await eagerly your return to the culmination of time. But in the meantime, I commit myself to personify hope in the world until the trumpet's blast. Come, Lord Jesus, come!

Notes

Chapter 1
1. George Keith, "How Firm a Foundation" (1787). Public domain.

Chapter 2
1. Francis Thompson, "The Hound of Heaven" (1893). Public domain.
2. Richard Chenevix Trench, "Prayer," in *Masterpieces of Religious Verse*, ed., James Dalton Morrison (New York: Harper & Row Publishers, 1948), p. 403.
3. "Seven Steps to Stagnation" (Chicago: Robert H. Franke Assn.).

Chapter 3
1. Frank Mason North, "Where Cross the Crowded Ways" and Charles Wesley, "Love Divine, All Loves Excelling." Public domain.
2. Public domain.

Chapter 4
1. William Cowper (1731-1800), "God Moves in a Mysterious Way." Public domain.
2. Hilton Oswald, *Luther's Works, Isaiah* (St. Louis: Concordia Publishing House, 1975), vol. 17, p. 393.
3. Author unknown.

Chapter 5
1. TOMORROW fr. "Annie" lyric: Martin Charnin; music: Charles Strouse. © 1977 EDWIN H. MORRIS & COMPANY, A Division of MPL Communications, Inc. & CHARLES STROUSE. International Copyright Secured. All Rights Reserved. Used by permission.
2. Horatius Bonar. No other information available.
3. From "He Touched Me" by William J. Gaither. © 1963 by William J. Gaither/ASCAP. All rights reserved. International copyright secured. Reprinted by special permission of The Benson Company, Inc., Nashville.

Chapter 7
1. Leslie D. Weatherhead, *In Quest of a Kingdom* (New York: Abingdon-Cokesbury Press), p. 138.